The Journey
THROUGH MIDDLE SCHOOL MATH

Karen Mayfield-Ingram
with Alma Ramirez

Illustrated by Ann Humphrey Williams
Produced by Louise Lang

THE JOURNEY—THROUGH MIDDLE SCHOOL MATH

About EQUALS

The mission of EQUALS is to improve mathematics education for *all* students. We have a special focus on making math accessible to females, students of color, and children from bilingual and low-income families. EQUALS develops innovative curriculum materials to help children everywhere experience success in mathematics.

As leaders in the field of mathematics, equity, and bilingual education, our academic staff present workshops as well as write books for home and classroom use.

Our website at www.lawrencehallofscience.org/equals contains information on EQUALS, our publications including FAMILY MATH books, and how we assist educators and families all over the world.

Complete contact information is below:

University of California, Berkeley
EQUALS Publications
Lawrence Hall of Science, #5200
Berkeley, CA 94720-5200

510.642.1823 — program
800.897.5036 or 510.642.1910 — books
510.643.5757 — fax
equals@berkeley.edu — program email
eqs_pubs@berkeley.edu — publications email

Credits:
Production Managers: Louise Lang and Karen Mayfield-Ingram
Cover and Principal Artist: Ann Humphrey Williams
Senior Editor: Kay Fairwell
Design: Carol Bevilacqua
Photographer: Elizabeth Crews

ISBN-13: 978-0-912511-31-3
ISBN-10: 0-912511-31-1

Printing (last digit) 10, 9, 8, 7, 6, 5, 4, 3, 2, 1

TABLE OF CONTENTS

TABLE OF CONTENTS

Acknowledgments

The authors of *The Journey—Through Middle School Math* would like to acknowledge many for their advice, support, and encouragement.

The Family Advocacy in Mathematics Education (FAME) program was funded through the *Lucent Technologies Foundation*. This funding supported the development, piloting, and publication of this book and its Spanish counterpart, *El Viaje—Por la matemática de la escuela secundaria.*

Inspiration for this book began during the writing of its predecessor, *FAMILY MATH—The Middle School Years, Algebraic Reasoning and Number Sense,* funded by the Dana Foundation of New York. We honor Virginia Thompson, Founding Director of the FAMILY MATH program, who passionately encouraged ALL parents to advocate for their children's mathematics success. Virginia created a foundation for every parent advocacy program to build upon.

We would like to thank the teachers and parents at Winton and Chavez Middle Schools and Tyrell Elementary School in Hayward, California for their involvement in pilot testing the FAME activities. In particular we would like to thank Gloria Prada, Richard Elliott, Chet Lloyd, Cherilee Heard, Carla Dardon, Mimi Deverse, Gina Croth, Alex Ramirez, Sean Moffatt, Sid Haro, and other Chavez staff. Kathy Barrett and Shiyon Bradford from the TEAMS program were wonderful in providing support during the development phases of the project.

EQUALS Site Directors Eleanor Linn and Steve Jordan were instrumental in the development of materials by providing feedback on the activities and FAME session model. Beverly Braxton, longtime EQUALS associate, and Grace Dávila Coates, FAMILY MATH Director, contributed several ingenious ideas for activities that appear in this book.

We appreciate Ann Barter's numerous contributions to the evaluation and development of activities and her endless commitment to the goals of the project. Celia Stevenson's creative illustrations and formatting enhanced the trial testing phase of the project. We are thankful that we connected with our old EQUALS friend.

We thank José Franco, Director of EQUALS, for providing ideas, insights, and encouragement throughout the development and production process. Louise Lang's creativity and vision provided us with a road map to follow throughout the production process. We will always be appreciative of her dedication. Terri Belcher's willingness to assist in the initial editing of this book is much appreciated. We were fortunate to have Carol Bevilacqua of the LHS Design Department creating an innovative format. As always, we find Ann Williams' cover art and illustrations irresistible.

We are grateful to the EQUALS staff who wholeheartedly supported the development and production of this book. They are Terri Belcher, Bob Capune, Grace Dávila Coates, Ellen Humm, José Franco, Louise Lang, Deborah Martinez, Oralia Ramirez, Claudia Sagastume, and Helen Raymond.

Karen Mayfield-Ingram
Principal Author

Alma Ramirez
Contributing Author

Beverly Braxton
Contributing Author

This Book Is About—

As parents, we want our children to have happy, fulfilling lives with more opportunities for success than we experienced. *The Journey—Through Middle School Math* helps families find their way through the unique challenges found in grades 5–8. Our goal is for your child to have a successful middle school mathematics experience that will maximize future career options.

Adolescence is marked developmentally by an increased ability to think abstractly. When children reach adolescence they are able to make many decisions for themselves. In fact, middle school children often spend a great deal of time telling their parents that they can handle their own lives and that they no longer need our guidance and supervision.

It is true that middle school children can make many decisions for themselves, and they should. However, there are some decisions that are too important for children to make by themselves. The stakes are too high. Our children may not have the ability to understand the long-term consequences of a decision.

Decisions made at the middle school level especially require parents' attention. Mathematics choices can greatly impact a child's high school course options and subsequent college opportunities. Important considerations should be discussed with children, but parents must make the final decisions.

This book contains advocacy and mathematics activities, and information for your family to enjoy together at home. We've highlighted a few significant elements along your middle school journey. However, each family must create its own unique path. We hope this book enables you and your child to find a way to informed decisions and successful mathematics experiences.

How to Use This Book–

This book is a map for finding your way through middle school.

Section One: Parent Advocacy
Section One is about advocating for your child. By advocacy, we mean parents taking actions to optimize a child's middle school experiences.

Parent advocacy activities address how to:
- Connect with your child's teachers
- Help your child with homework
- Bridge home and school
- Understand test results and their influence
- Choose math courses that increase career options

To better assist your family on this journey, the advocacy activities and information are placed in a suggested sequence. This sequence corresponds to the school year. However, while each activity builds on the other, all were designed to stand alone.

Most of the activities in the advocacy section are for parents and children to do together. We suggest that you read the activity and then do it with your child. It will be important to discuss the information that you learn. Take time to share each other's perspectives.

Section Two: Algebra and Geometry Activities

These two math concepts introduce students to higher mathematics and are stumbling blocks for many children.

Algebra is required for many disciplines such as biology, sociology, psychology, and economics. Geometry is usually the second course children take after algebra. Many high school exit exams and other college entrance tests focus on algebra and geometry.

Throughout the mathematics section, you and your child will explore key algebra and geometry concepts. Each activity has easy-to-follow instructions. See the Sample Math Activity Page on pages 70–71.

When you and your child investigate the math activities, we suggest that you begin by discussing "Why is this important?" Take turns reading each activity aloud. Talk about the mathematics involved as you follow the instructions. Encourage each other's thinking by asking questions as you move through each activity. Go at a pace that is comfortable for you and your child.

To assist your math explorations, we included answers for certain problems. Right answers are important; however, understanding **why** an answer is correct is equally important.

We hope the design of this book gives you and your family a clear and useful road map through middle school mathematics.

How Can I Help My Child Succeed with Homework?

BRIDGING HOME & SCHOOL

Helping our children with homework can be a difficult thing. We don't do it like the teacher, or it is too hard for us. As parents, we are not expected to teach the content that is covered in our children's math classes. However, we play an extremely important role in helping our children succeed with their homework.

Sometimes, when our children struggle, our first instinct is to say, "Maybe you need to sit closer to the front," or "Are you sure you are paying close attention in class?"

There are other kinds of questions we can pose. We as parents and caregivers can learn to ask the kinds of questions that allow children to think through problems themselves. This will also enable us to see how our child is thinking mathematically.

Questions List
- Let's see. What do you know right now?
- What steps did you take?
- Is there a pattern you can follow?
- Can we work through one of the problems that you did understand?
- Did you check your arithmetic?

Middle school mathematics builds on the foundation developed in elementary school. For many students, the homework may seem easy. For others it might be difficult, especially if they struggled with elementary mathematics.

Regardless of where our children fall, it is crucial that we stress the importance of reviewing and revising homework before beginning other activities. Doing homework needs to take a higher priority than playing video games, chatting with friends on the phone, or watching television. If children understand that homework is important to do first, they are more likely to take it seriously.

Parents and children can look at homework together to make sure the assignment is complete. Children often need repeated encouragement to revise their homework. Remember, you do not have to be an expert in order to help your child. Here are some additional questions you can use:

- Can you show me how you worked this problem out?
- Is there anything you forgot to do?
- How do you know that your answers are correct?
- Do your answers make sense?

What else can I do to help my child with homework?

There are other things we can do to help our children succeed in math class. Here are some ideas.

- **Visit your child's math teacher**

  We might ask our children's teacher to show us what the expectations are for completing homework. We can ask for examples of excellent homework and unacceptable homework so that we can help our children understand what is expected.

- **Ask more questions**

  Throughout this book, we have included additional questions that we might use when working with our children.

- **Talk with your child**

  It is important that our children realize that we don't know everything. We can talk to our children about our own school experiences. We can ask our children to explain to us what they understand about a particular homework assignment and what is troublesome. We have to let children know we are rooting for them. We are their biggest advocates!

- **Provide a consistent time and place for homework**

  This might seem difficult, especially if we work late hours or have other children in the house. However, it is very important that our children recognize that homework is a priority. If we work late, we can call our child at a specified time and ask about the homework assignments. If we have other children at home, we can make homework a family time by providing coloring books to preschoolers and asking younger students to also do their homework. It is advisable to keep stereos and televisions off during homework time.

What if I don't understand the mathematics homework that my child brings home?

This is a more common problem than many of us think. Lots of parents have never taken algebra or an advanced math class. Our children's assignments may seem totally out of our reach. If so, there are resources available to help children succeed with homework.

• Seek out tutorial services

Many schools have homework clubs, computer clubs, and other after-school programs. You can check to see if your child's school has an after-school math/science program, such as the Mathematics, Engineering, Science Achievement (MESA), or Upward Bound programs. Many of these programs work through local colleges and universities, are free of charge, and will assist our children in math and other areas.

• Seek out community resources

Many churches and community centers have clubs where children can get assistance with their homework. There are also publications available from district offices, state departments of education, and the United States Department of Education. All of these are only a phone call away.

• Seek out Internet resources

Not all of us have computers at home. Even so, computer access is becoming easier than ever. Libraries, community centers, and even computer resource rooms at schools allow parents to use computers. There are online math tutors available. Some offer math resources that can be purchased and are available in different languages. A few are listed below:

http://www.mathpower.com

http://www.homeworkspot.com

http://www.kidsmath.com

What Do We Value?

MATERIALS
pencil
Value List, page 5

Why is this important?
It is vital for families to talk about what they, as individuals, value regarding education, social interactions, work habits, achievement expectations, and future career options.

Middle school children go through many changes. They explore new ideas and formulate opinions that may differ from their parents' views. Misunderstandings can very easily occur between parents and children.

Understanding values allows parents and children to voice their perspectives on many issues such as peer interactions, educational goals, and career dreams.

This activity is a vehicle for parents and their children to share what they each value.

How
  • Duplicate the Value List, one copy for each person.

  • Write your name at the top of your list.

  • Work independently and read through the list.

  • Place a check next to the top 10 things you value.

  • Now go back over the list and circle the 5 things you value most.

  • Trade lists with each other.

  • Look at what was marked. Note similarities and differences.

  • Allow time for everybody to discuss their value list. Be curious but not judgmental. Encourage each person to talk about the choices made.

  • What surprising things did you learn about yourself and others in your family?

Value List

Being respected

Having my (friends or child) think that I am fair

Accomplishing my dreams

Fitting in with my peers

Having a great career

Being competitive

Reading

Making friends

Eating my favorite foods

Being liked

Managing time

Doing extreme sports

Feeling loved

Going to college

Having a family

Learning new things

Playing sports

Asking questions when I do not know

Making money

Being a leader

Making my own decisions

Persisting in work

Being organized

Playing music

Feeling safe

Questioning what I have been taught

Traveling

Solving problems skillfully

Volunteering my time

Making good grades

Being patient

Here's More...

Come up with 5 things that you value that were not on this list. Discuss them with your family.

Connecting with Your Child's Teachers

BRIDGING HOME & SCHOOL

Think back to your own school years. Did your parents know how to connect with your teachers when you transferred to middle school? Did your parents only interact with your teachers when there was a problem?

Research shows that children with involved parents experience higher academic success. The benefits of parent involvement are not limited to early childhood programs or the elementary grades. Studies show that active parents can positively impact their children's education through high school and beyond.

There is also evidence that children learn best when teachers and parents work together. This is why it is important that you have a good working relationship with your child's teachers.

Sometimes teachers reach out first, but we can share the responsibility for creating and maintaining strong parent/teacher communication. What are some ways to connect with your child's teachers?

- Introduce yourself in person at the start of the school year. Let the teachers know that you will be contacting them on a regular basis to discuss your child's progress. Ask the teachers how they prefer to be contacted—by telephone, email, or by letter. Indicate how you prefer to be contacted.

- Ask each teacher how your child's performance will be evaluated. This is best accomplished at the beginning of the year. Find out how teachers will prioritize homework, classroom participation, and test scores.

- Discuss with your child's teachers how decisions are made at school. Are important policies decided by the school staff? How are parent voices included in the decision-making process?

- Be appreciative when teachers enrich your child's experiences in learning. Let a teacher know when your child is excited about a project, lesson, or field trip.

- If you disagree with one of your child's teachers, avoid criticizing the teacher in front of your child. First make an appointment with the teacher to clarify the issues. If you cannot reach a satisfactory solution, follow up with a conference including other school personnel. Children need to see successful problem solving between parents and teachers.

Consistent communication will enable you to:
- stay better informed about your child's progress.
- create a strong partnership with your child's teachers.

Remember—to reach their highest potential, children need advocates. Parents and teachers working together make the strongest advocates.

Key Contacts at School

BRIDGING HOME AND SCHOOL

Getting familiar with middle school procedures and policies can be daunting. Knowing who is in charge of various responsibilities at your child's school is important.

The following pages contain templates to help you sort through the middle school maze. Some of the information can be gathered from notices, newsletters, conversations with other parents; or by talking with your child. Take a minute to complete the pages. It may be helpful to tear them out and place them in a more convenient place such as in a binder, or on your refrigerator door or a bulletin board.

Your Child's TEACHERS Reference sheet

Teachers	Name	Telephone # & ext.	email	Room #	Responsibilities	Comments
Math Teacher						
Mathematics Department Chair						
Class Advisor						
Other Teachers by Subject						

Class visitation policy:

Your child's SCHOOL Reference Sheet

Your School Staff	Name	Telephone # & ext.	email	Room #	Responsibilities	Comments
Principal						
Vice Principal(s)						
Student Supervisor/Dean						
Secretary or Administrative Assistant						
Resource Teachers: Bilingual Education Special Education Federal and State Special Projects						
Community Liaison						
Counselor(s)						

School visitation policy:

Your child's SCHOOL DISTRICT Reference Sheet

District Administration	Name	Telephone # & ext.	email	Room #	Responsibilities	Comments
Superintendent						
Associate Superintendent— Curriculum & Instruction						
Categorical Funds						
School Board Members:						

How Do We Handle It?

BRIDGING HOME AND SCHOOL

Why is it important?

As with any relationship, there are times when differences of opinion and miscommunication occur. This is particularly true in relationships between schools and families. When issues arise, it's useful to have specific strategies in mind to help you navigate to a satisfactory solution.

This activity is designed to give parents time to think about typical middle school interactions. The following scenarios are real; middle school parents shared them with us. However, the names have been changed.

Read each vignette with your child. Talk with your child or other parents about possible solutions to these situations. Remember, there is often more than one path to a solution. What would you do if your family had to face these issues? Use the Options for Advocacy Chart on page 16 to write down some of your ideas.

MATERIALS

Vignette #1: Options for Advocacy Chart, page 16
pen or pencil

Vignette #1

My daughter, Claudia, was always a good student. She always got high grades. When they put her in the algebra class everything changed. Claudia would cry before every math test. A couple of times she even got sick. She struggled with her homework and failed all the tests.

When I spoke to her teacher, he told me all she did in class was talk. He told me there were three other girls in the class and none of them worked very hard. He said, "Middle school girls go through these phases."

I talked to my daughter about how she felt and acted in class. Claudia told me that the teacher just went too fast, and she often felt stupid when she asked a question. Claudia felt the teacher got impatient with her for asking anything and the other kids would laugh. So Claudia stopped asking questions, thinking that if she tried harder and listened more closely, things would get better.

I hired a math tutor that really strained our budget. I just wanted my daughter to do well. Her tutor told me that Claudia understood everything and her homework was always correct. But her homework only counted for 20 percent of her grade, and the tests were 80 percent.

By the time the first semester ended, her teacher recommended that Claudia be transferred into something called Math B. I found out that two of the other girls are also leaving the algebra class. I don't think any boys were bumped back. I don't know what to do any more.

Vignette #1 Discussion

This mother is very concerned about her daughter's success in school. She has already done many things to advocate for her child.

- She talked to her daughter.

  Talking to our children in a supportive way is very important. This lets them know that we are there to help them through their struggles. Children need to know that their parents value their point of view, and this mom listened to her daughter's perspective. Students this age need to feel some degree of independence and control over their lives, even though they still depend on their parents for guidance and help. It is also important that middle school students begin to take responsibility for their academic success.

- She talked to her daughter's teacher as soon as she realized there was a problem.

  This is a wise second step. It is hard for many parents to talk to teachers. For the sake of our children's success, parents and teachers need to work together.

- She sought outside help.

  Even though it strained the family's budget, this mother chose to hire a tutor to help Claudia. This may not be a possibility for all parents. There are often free tutorial services offered through community centers, after-school homework clubs, or even tutoring websites. Parents might also consider enrolling their child in student outreach programs. The goal is to be resourceful when seeking help for our children.

  There may be other options available to this mom and her daughter. What would you do? Here are some questions to help you get started. Use the chart entitled Vignette 1: Options for Advocacy on page16 to record your thoughts.

• What is taught in a Math B class, and how is it different from an algebra class?

• What are things that this family can do to build Claudia's confidence in math?

• If this mom talked with other parents, how might these conversations help?

• How might this mother prepare for a second meeting with the teacher?

• What are the advantages of asking for a parent/teacher conference with the principal?

• If other options fail, what key issues would you discuss with the superintendent or the school board?

Math B was designed as a middle school course. It is taught at the eighth or ninth grade level. The specific content may vary with each district but it generally covers material from several math areas, e.g., number and operations, algebra, geometry, probability, measurement and data analysis. Students who are not ready for an algebra course often enroll in Math B.

Vignette 1: Options for Advocacy Chart

Talk with your partner about each of the following questions, and record key ideas.

Question	Key Ideas
What is taught in a Math B class, and how is it different from an algebra class?	
What are things that this family can do to build Claudia's confidence in math?	
If this mom talked with other parents, how might these conversations help?	
How might this mother prepare for a second meeting with the teacher?	
What are the advantages of asking for a parent/teacher conference with the principal?	
If other options fail, what key issues would you discuss with the superintendent or the school board?	

My wife and I work different shifts so our three kids don't need to be in after-school care. We feel that middle school is a risky time to leave kids unattended. My wife picks them up from school, makes dinner, and then leaves for work an hour after I get home. I feed the children dinner and help them with their homework. I also put our two-year-old to bed. This doesn't leave me a lot of time to go to school functions.

The other day I found a crumpled note in my daughter's backpack about a parent conference we missed. In my son's backpack, I found an old flyer about a FAMILY MATH night we also missed. It's not like we don't want to be involved. What am I supposed to do with the baby when I have to go to school functions or meetings? What if I have to meet with my son's teacher? Do I take the other two children with me?

It bothers me when people say that parents who don't show up at school don't care about their kids' education. A lot of us want to be involved but can't afford extra childcare.

Vignette #2 Discussion

Sound familiar? Lots of us struggle when making choices between work and family. Many of us feel like we do not have many options. This father wants to be involved but is juggling work and caring for three children.

Below are some options to think and talk about with your partner.

- Ask your children about what's going on at school.

    Kids are notorious for not giving parents school flyers or bringing notes home. They frequently tell us about school functions on the day of the event, and this can cause last-minute stress.

    On a regular basis, ask your children what is going on at school. Ask if there is anything in their backpacks such as school flyers, parent meeting announcements, or course information forms.

- Talk to the teacher, principal, or counselor about childcare options.

    Schools sometimes provide childcare when there are parent meetings or functions. Remember that siblings are often allowed to come with their parents for events like Open House or FAMILY MATH nights.

• Find or create a parent support group.

Talking and meeting with other parents to build a support group opens many possibilities. Parents often can be the best resources. Getting to know the parents of your child's classmates can be very beneficial now and in the future. For example, parents can take turns babysitting for the younger siblings so that more parents can attend school events.

Another strength of a parent network is sharing valuable information and recommendations on school issues. Parents can talk about math course options their children should consider.

Vignette #3

Typically an algebra course is covered in a year.

In order to address the difficulty many students are experiencing in algebra, many middle schools have divided the algebra course into two parts—Algebra A and Algebra B. Students in Algebra A spend an entire year on half the content and, if they pass the course, they take Algebra B in high school. The specific content in each part can vary with each district.

See Math Journey to High School *on page 20 for more information on course enrollment options.*

Pamela lives with her grandmother and is attending a new school. One day, her grandmother overhears some parents talking about next year's math classes. That night, Pamela gives her grandmother a paper from the teacher describing next year's math courses. There are two options—Algebra and Algebra A—and Algebra A is circled on the paper.

Pamela's grandmother is confused and asks what the difference is between the two classes. Pamela says, "I don't know. All the smart kids are going into Algebra. It's too hard for me. Ms. Phillips said because of my math scores I'd do better in Algebra A."

Pamela's grandmother is puzzled and has questions:

• Which is the higher course, Algebra or Algebra A?

• What does the "A" in Algebra A stand for?

• Is it better to be in a lower math class and get a higher grade or be in a higher math class and get a lower grade?

• Which class will be better for Pamela if she wants to go to college?

Pamela's grandmother doesn't want to push her too hard. Pamela has already made many difficult adjustments at this new school. Algebra A is still algebra, isn't it?

Vignette #3 Discussion

Sometimes it's very difficult to know how hard to push our children academically. When is a course too hard? What is best overall for a child? Information from schools can be confusing. Where do we go for answers?

Using the discussion information below, how would you help Pamela's grandmother answer her questions and decide what to do?

- In preparation for a meeting with a teacher, talk with your child.
  All children want to feel successful in school. Unfortunately, children often equate difficulty with failure, and ease with success. If they are struggling in a course, they assume that it is too difficult for them and may choose to be in a lower level course. It's important to talk with your children to determine if they are experiencing frustration with courses and, if so, how much frustration. We all experience frustration as we grow and learn.

  In addition, children often want to be with their friends. However, using friendship as the indicator for enrollment in a math course is not wise. Friends may or may not share the same interest, performance, and persistence level. Course decisions need to be made based on what's right for each child.

- Make an appointment with the math teacher.
  Names of math courses can be confusing to parents. Teachers and administrators design them. Often the course names do not fully indicate what the content is or the course level.

  Make an appointment with your child's math teacher early in the year. Discuss the content of the course, what the other course options are, and how the courses feed into the high school's college preparatory courses. Having this information can assist you in determining which math course is appropriate for your child.

- Connect with other parents in your child's class.
  Talking with other parents can provide insight into your own child's experiences. It may be a bit daunting to ask others for information, particularly in new situations. However, most parents when approached will happily share their perspectives and information. You will probably find that other parents have similar concerns. Perhaps they have dealt with a related experience in the past and found a resolution that will help you.

Math Journey to High School

IS YOUR CHILD COLLEGE BOUND?

Algebra has a gatekeeper role in mathematics course selection and, consequently, college and career options.

The following table outlines standard mathematics course sequences from middle school to high school. The sequence assumes that a student has achieved a passing grade in the previous course. The titles of the courses may vary. It is important to talk with your child's counselor or mathematics department chair for the specific titles and course content used in your school.

Algebra and Algebra A/B

Typically an algebra course is covered in a year. In order to address the difficulty many students are experiencing in algebra, however, many middle schools have divided the algebra course into two parts—Algebra A and Algebra B. Students in Algebra A spend an entire year on half the content and, if they pass the course, take Algebra B in high school. The specific content in each part can vary with each district.

Math B

Math B was designed as a middle school course. It is taught at the 8th or 9th grade levels. The specific content may vary with each district, but it generally covers material from several math areas, e.g., number and operations, algebra, geometry, probability, and measurement and data analysis. Students who are not ready for an algebra course often enroll in Math B.

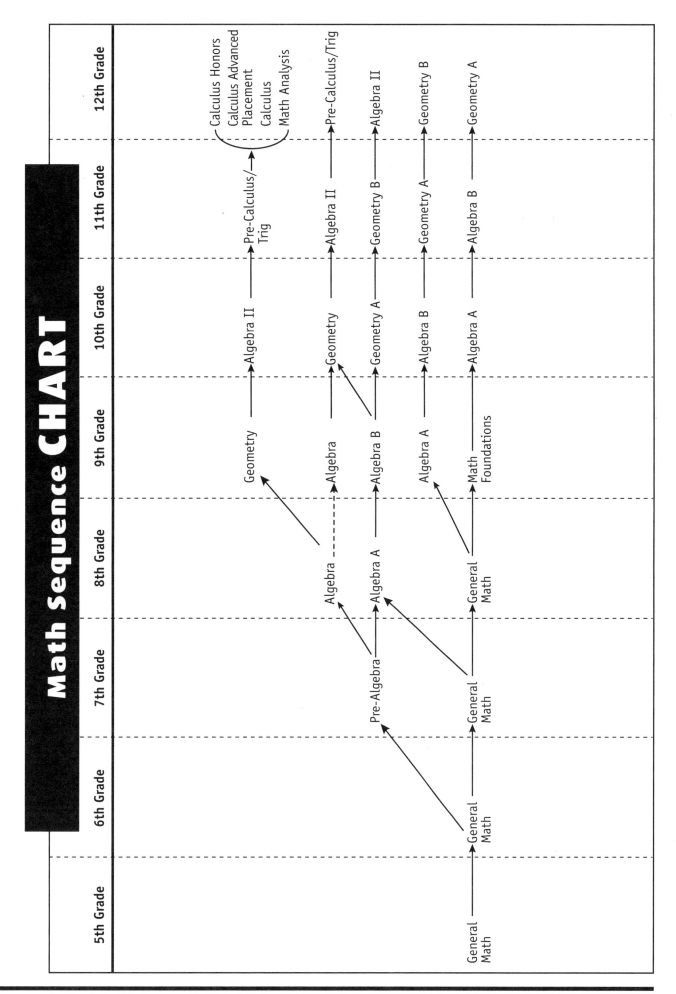

Math Sequence CHART

	5th Grade	6th Grade	7th Grade	8th Grade	9th Grade	10th Grade	11th Grade	12th Grade
	General Math	General Math	Pre-Algebra	Algebra	Geometry	Algebra II	Pre-Calculus/Trig	Math Analysis Calculus Calculus Advanced Placement Calculus Honors
				Algebra A	Algebra B	Geometry	Algebra II	Pre-Calculus/Trig
					Algebra B	Geometry A	Geometry B	Algebra II
			General Math	General Math	Algebra A	Algebra B	Geometry A	Geometry B
					Math Foundations	Algebra A	Algebra B	Geometry A

One of the major changes in the course sequence at the middle school level is the inclusion of all students in an algebra course. Traditionally, most children began formal algebra instruction in the 9th grade. A select few were allowed to take algebra in 8th grade. Concerns regarding achievement and equity prompted support for the course to be taught at the 8th grade level to all students.

A 1996 international mathematics study (Third International Mathematics and Science Study) found that students in the United States were less prepared than students in other countries. The reason for this achievement disparity was the course tracking at the middle school level. The study revealed that not enough children were taking higher-level math courses. The information from other countries reinforced what many in the United States had believed—all students should be able to take algebra in the 8th grade.

Many four year colleges and universities require at least three years of mathematics for admission. However, to be competitive at many universities, high school students need four years of mathematics including calculus. In other words, your child must begin algebra in the 8th grade in order to take calculus in the 12th grade. It is possible to double up math courses or attend summer school, but this is difficult for most children.

Changing Quarters

STANDARDIZED TESTING

MATERIALS
- **Scoreboard, page 28**
- **Tiles, page 29**
- **Record Sheet, page 30**

Why is this important?
Standardized tests are the most commonly used evaluation tool in education. Have you ever found your child's test scores confusing? It is important to understand how to interpret these scores.

It is generally assumed that test scores measure how much a child knows. This is not always the case. The test reporting system is complex and one that some parents and educators do not fully understand.

In this activity, we'll learn how a frequently used type of score (percentile) is calculated and what it tells us. You will be working with student scores from a standardized test given to a class of 15 middle-school students. There were 100 questions on the test.

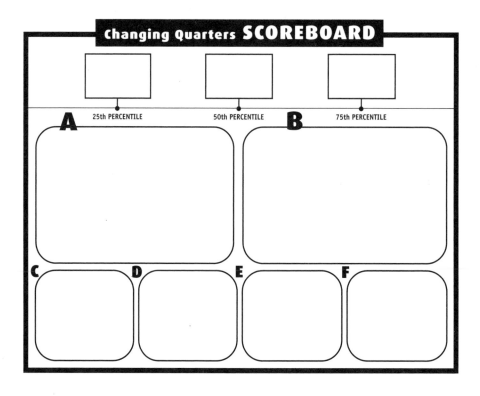

Changing Quarters SCOREBOARD

A   25th PERCENTILE   50th PERCENTILE   B   75th PERCENTILE

C   D   E   F

How

• Cut out Round 1 test score tiles on page 29. Place them in a row in numerical order. Discuss the set of test scores you just arranged. What can you say about them?

• Using the Scoreboard, take the lowest test score (13) and place it in group A. Take the highest score (80) from the other end of the row and place it in group B.

• The illustration below shows you how to sort the remaining tiles into Groups A and B. Sort the tiles by alternately placing the lowest remaining score in Group A and the highest remaining score in Group B. Continue until you have used all the scores.

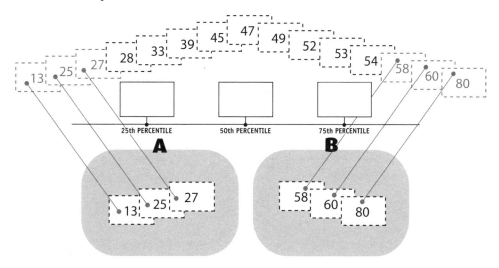

• There will be an equal number of tiles in each group with one left over (47). The leftover tile is called the middle or median score.

• Place the median score (47) in the 50th percentile box on the Scoreboard. Looking at the illustration below, what else can you say about the test scores of this middle-school class?

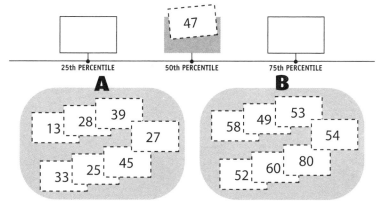

• One thing you can say is that half of the remaining students scored higher than 47 (the median score) and half of the remaining students scored lower than 47.

• Now we want to find the median among the scores to the left of the 50th percentile. Place the score tiles from Group A in numerical order. Sort them into groups C and D, alternating from the beginning and end of the row as you did before.

• You will have 1 tile left over. Place that score (28) in the 25th percentile box.

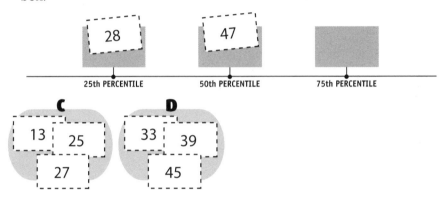

• What can you say about the student who received a score of 28? How does that child's score compare to others in the class? Did you discover that this child scored lower than 75% of all the students and higher than 25%?

• What can you say about the student who scored 45? Or 27?

• Now we want to find the median among the scores to the right of the 50th percentile mark. You will be working with the score tiles from group B.

• Arrange the scores in numerical order and sort them into groups E and F. What number represents the middle score of this set?

• Place the leftover score tile (54) in the 75th percentile box.

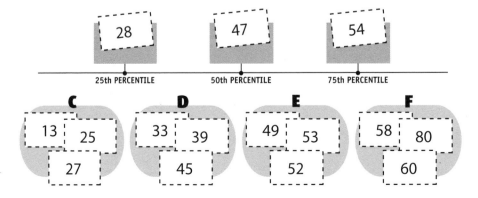

- What can you say about the student who scored 54? If you look at the test scores for all 15 students, what do you notice? Discuss this with your child or others in the group.
- Your final step for Round 1 is to record the 25th, 50th, and 75th percentile scores. Use the record sheet on page 30.
- Now go through the same process for Rounds 2 and 3.

More questions for discussion

- If your child scored 54 in all three rounds, describe what that would mean. Would you be satisfied in each case? What about a score of 47 or 66?
- What do you now know about test scores that are reported as percentiles?

Here's More...

- The next time a standardized test is scheduled, ask your child's teacher the purpose of the test, how the test will be used, and how to help your child prepare.

- Once the test is over and you receive your child's test results, ask your child's teacher the significance of the scores. Clarify how many problems were on the test and how many your child answered correctly. Find out how your child's performance ranked among others in the class, the school, the state, and the nation. Discuss next steps with the teacher.

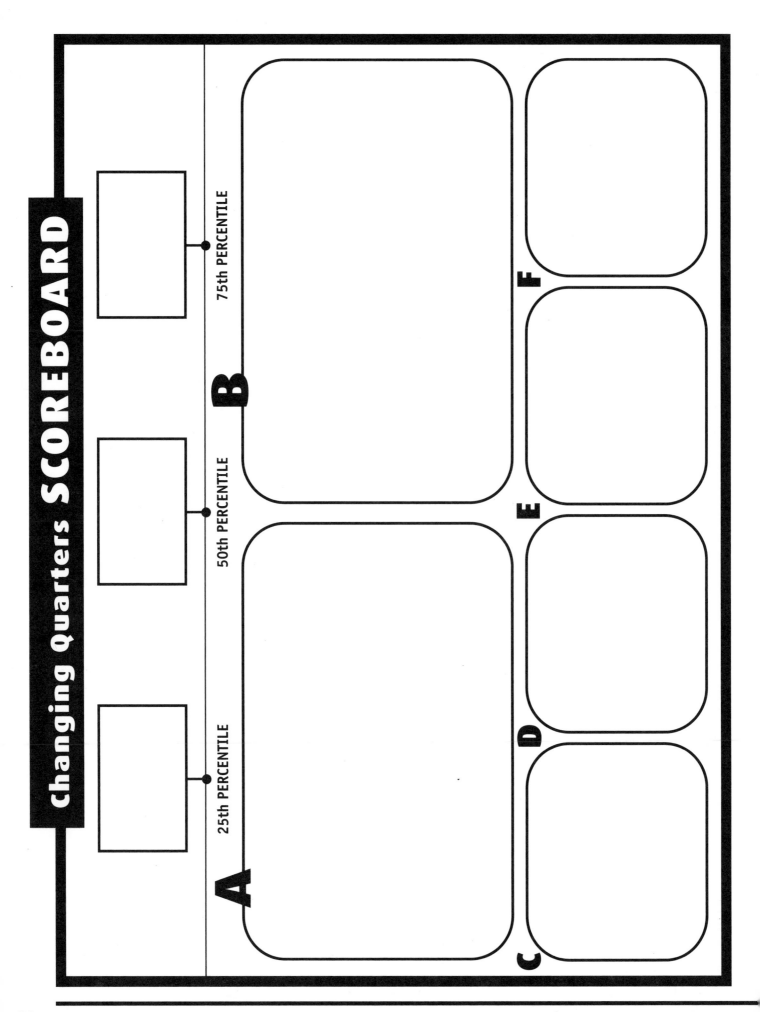

changing Quarters **SCOREBOARD**

25th PERCENTILE

50th PERCENTILE

75th PERCENTILE

A

B

C

D

E

F

Changing Quarters Test Score TILES

ROUND 1

13	25	27	28	33
39	45	47	49	52
53	54	58	60	80

ROUND 2

25	27	28	32	33
39	40	41	44	45
45	47	54	57	83

ROUND 3

15	19	22	24	27
28	30	31	40	54
63	66	74	85	92

Changing Quarters RECORD SHEET

Record the 25th, 50th, and 75th percentile scores for all three rounds as indicated below.

	25th PERCENTILE	50th PERCENTILE	75th PERCENTILE
ROUND 1			
ROUND 2			
ROUND 3			

Getting Out of High School

MATERIALS

Puzzle, page 35

scissors

paper

pencils

High School Exit Exam
  Puzzle Chart, page 34

PUTTING THE EXIT EXAM PUZZLE TOGETHER

HIGH SCHOOL EXIT EXAM

Why is this important?

Many states have adopted an exit exam for high school students. Exit exams measure achievement in mathematics and language arts. The rationale for an exit exam is based on the fact that some students are graduating without the necessary skills and knowledge to do well in a job or succeed in college. Exit exams are meant to provide more credibility to a high school diploma.

Most states require this exam be taken in the 10th or 11th grades. Families who learn about the content early will gain a better opportunity for their children's success.

In the following activity, you and your child will assemble a puzzle with pieces that contain information on the California High School Exit Exam (CAHSEE). We selected California because many other states use its curriculum and assessments as a model for developing their own programs.

How
- Make a copy of the puzzle on page 35, and cut out the pieces.

- Ask your child to read aloud the information on each piece while assembling the puzzle.

- What surprises did you and your child find?

- Make notes from your discussion on the High School Exit Exam Puzzle Chart on page 34.

- Talk with your child's math and English teachers about the exit exam. Early in the school year, ask for additional resources to help prepare your child for this test.

Here's More...
- For current information on the high school exit exam in your state, find your Department of Education's website and search under student assessment or accountability.

Write in your answers below.

What purpose does the exit exam serve?

What is the content of the test?

What happens if a student does not pass?

How is it scored?

When and who has to take the test?

Purpose of the High School Exit Exam

Ensures that high school graduates can demonstrate competence in reading, writing, and mathematics based on state content standards.

Sample question

$x^3y^3 =$
$$\underline{}\ \underline{}\ \underline{}$$

a. 9xy
b. (xy)6
c. 3xy
d. xxxyyy

The answer is d or xxxyyy.

What support is available if a student does not pass?

Districts must provide supplemental instruction to assist those who do not pass the exam. This includes summer school for seniors.

Where can I find current exam info for California?

For more information www.cde.ca.gov/statetests/cahsee For other states, contact the state's Department of Education.

What lies ahead?

Advanced algebra and geometry may be added in future years.

Sample question

The points (1, 1), (2, 3), (4, 3), and (5, 1) are the vertices of a polygon. What type of polygon is formed by these points?

a. Triangle   c. Parallelogram
b. Trapezoid   d. Pentagon

The answer is b.

When is the exam given?

All 10th grade students are required to take the test in the spring. Students may be given up to 5 additional opportunities to retake the sections not passed.

Is the exam given in several languages?

No. All English Language Learners are required to take the exam in English.

Math content

Content is based on grades 6 and 7 and Algebra I standards.

What is a passing score?

To pass the exam, a student needs to correctly answer approximately 55% of the math questions and 60% of the English language arts questions.

Exam format

All questions are multiple-choice. No calculators are allowed.

Math topics

Math topics covered include: number sense, statistics, data analysis, probability, measurement, geometry, and Algebra 1 content.

Math and Your Child's Career Options

MATH AND CAREERS

We recommend that your family play "Odds On You" Revisited on page 50 before you begin this activity.

We recommend that your family play "Odds On You" Revisited on page 50

MATERIALS

Job Cards, pages 38–42
Career Options Chart,
 page 43
Highlighted Job
 Descriptions and Salaries,
 pages 44-48

Why is this important?

Many jobs and careers require more mathematics than you might expect. It is important to start thinking about your child's future math courses early on. The middle school years are a good time to discuss careers with your child. This activity demonstrates the impact of high school math courses on career options.

Preparation

• Cut out the job cards, and place them in an envelope.

How

• Write each of the following four categories on a separate piece of paper or sticky note pad such as a Post-it.

 A. 4 Years High School Math Required (calculus and more)
 B. 3–4 Years High School Math Recommended
 C. 2 Years High School Math Required
 D. 2 Years High School Math Recommended

• Take a job card. Talk about the level of high school mathematics you think is necessary to begin preparation for that job. For example, if you select the veterinarian job card, talk about what veterinarians do and the mathematics they use in their jobs. Then discuss the high school math courses that a student needs to take to prepare for that career. Place the veterinarian job card under the category that you think is the best match.

- Continue the process for the other job cards. Choose and talk about as many job cards as you like. Don't forget to place them into one of the four categories.

- Look at the Career Options chart. How do your family's results compare with the chart?

- What are the similarities and differences among the jobs in each category? How do the jobs compare across categories?

- Which jobs interest your child and why? How much math is required for each? How might this information impact which math courses your child takes next year? In two years?

- What is the minimal amount of math required for high school graduation? What happens to your child's career options if your child takes more math in high school than required? Discuss this with your child.

- Take a look at Highlighted Job Descriptions and Salaries on pages 44–48, and discuss several from each category with your child. What surprises did you find?

Here's More...

- Were there any jobs that you were not familiar with? For example, what is an actuary? What does an actuary do? Where could you find out more information about the mathematics requirements of various careers?

- Ask your child to interview three people with jobs she finds interesting. What kinds of math does each person use?

- Collect and look at catalogs from community colleges, four-year colleges, and universities. You and your child may also find this information online. Pick a major course of study from each catalog, and find out how much math is required.

Career Job CARDS

Pharmacist	Architect	Geographer	Elementary Teacher
Public Health Nurse	Economist	Optometrist	Lawyer
Interior Designer	Dentist	Veterinarian	Registered Nurse
Pharmacy Assistant	Physician	Biologist	Urban Planner

Career Job CARDS

Engineer	Geologist	Accountant, Certified Public	Animal Care Technician
Physicist	Chemist	Electronic Technician	Cartographer/ Mapmaker
Sociologist	Astronomer	Occupational & Physical Therapist	Welder
Psychologist	Meteorologist	Speech Therapist	Health Record Administrator

Graphic Artist	Tool and Die Maker	Surveyor	Electrician
Computer Technologist	Bookkeeper	Property Appraiser	Actuary
Applied and Pure Mathematicians	Landscape Architect	Audiologist	Forester/ Conservation Scientist
Statistician	Agricultural Technician	Data Processor	Commercial Driver

Career Job CARDS

Cashier	College Math Professor	Building and Construction Inspector	Respiratory Technologist
Drafter	Math Teacher	Insurance Claims Clerk	Plumber
Mechanic	Biochemist	X-Ray Technician	Statistical Clerk
Carpenter	Stockbroker	Bricklayer/ Stonemason	Loan Checker

Career Job CARDS

Travel Agent	Aircraft Pilot & Flight Engineer	Cost Estimator	Operations Research Analyst
Bank Teller	Stock Clerk	Loan & Insurance Underwriter	Computer Systems Analyst
Jeweler	Mechanical Equipment Maintenance Technician	Computer Programmer	Electrical & Electronic Technician
Weigher, Measurer, Checker	Order Clerk	Dental Hygienist	Machinist

Career Options **Chart**

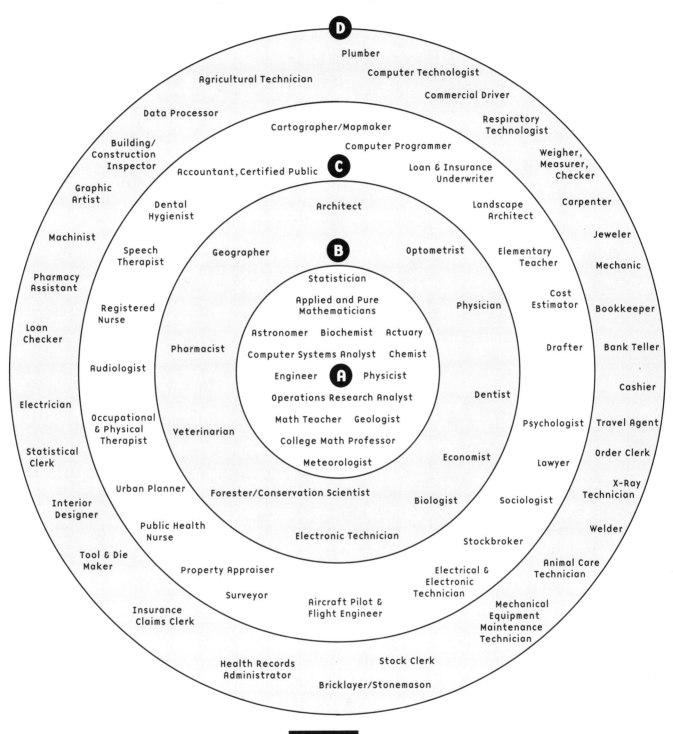

D

Plumber
Computer Technologist
Agricultural Technician
Commercial Driver
Data Processor
Respiratory Technologist
Building/ Construction Inspector
Cartographer/Mapmaker
Computer Programmer
Weigher, Measurer, Checker
C
Accountant, Certified Public
Loan & Insurance Underwriter
Graphic Artist
Architect
Landscape Architect
Carpenter
Dental Hygienist
B
Jeweler
Machinist
Geographer
Optometrist
Elementary Teacher
Mechanic
Speech Therapist
Statistician
Applied and Pure Mathematicians
Physician
Cost Estimator
Pharmacy Assistant
Bookkeeper
Registered Nurse
Astronomer   Biochemist   Actuary
Computer Systems Analyst   Chemist
Drafter
Bank Teller
Loan Checker
Pharmacist
Engineer   **A**   Physicist
Cashier
Operations Research Analyst
Dentist
Audiologist
Math Teacher   Geologist
Psychologist
Travel Agent
Electrician
Veterinarian
College Math Professor
Order Clerk
Occupational & Physical Therapist
Meteorologist
Economist
Lawyer
Statistical Clerk
Forester/Conservation Scientist
Biologist
Sociologist
X-Ray Technician
Urban Planner
Welder
Interior Designer
Public Health Nurse
Electronic Technician
Stockbroker
Tool & Die Maker
Property Appraiser
Electrical & Electronic Technician
Animal Care Technician
Surveyor
Aircraft Pilot & Flight Engineer
Insurance Claims Clerk
Mechanical Equipment Maintenance Technician
Health Records Administrator
Stock Clerk
Bricklayer/Stonemason

LEGEND

A. 4 Years High School Math Required (calculus and more)

B. 3–4 Years High School Math Recommended

C. 2 Years High School Math Required

D. 2 Years High School Math Recommended

HIGHLIGHTED JOB DESCRIPTIONS AND SALARIES IN THE UNITED STATES

Actuary I (Insurance)

Conducts analysis, pricing, and risk assessment to estimate financial outcomes. Develops evaluation and financial reporting standards. May require a bachelor's degree in a related field and 0–2 years of experience. Has knowledge of commonly used concepts, practices, and procedures within a particular field. Relies on instructions and pre-established guidelines to perform the functions of the job. Works under immediate supervision. Primary job functions do not typically require exercising independent judgment. Typically reports to a supervisor or manager.

A typical Actuary I earns a median base salary of $42,360.

Actuary I

25th percentile	Median	75th percentile
$37,848	$42,360	$46,409

Architect (Architecture)

Conceives, designs and constructs new or modified buildings or structures, such as private residences, office buildings, theaters, factories, and other structural property. Requires a bachelor's degree and 2–4 years of experience in the field or in a related area. Familiar with standard concepts, practices, and procedures within a particular field. Relies on experience and judgment to plan and accomplish goals. Performs a variety of complicated tasks. Works under general supervision; typically reports to a supervisor or manager. A certain degree of creativity and latitude is required.

A typical Architect earns a median base salary of $55,115.

Architect

25th percentile	Median	75th percentile
$47,401	$55,115	$65,126

Audiologist (Healthcare — Practitioners)

Administers and interprets a variety of tests, such as air and bone conduction, and speech reception and discrimination tests, to determine the type and degree of hearing impairment, site of damage, and effects on comprehension and speech. Evaluates test results in relation to behavioral, social, educational, and medical information obtained from patients, families, teachers, and other professionals. Requires a master's degree and a 9-month fellowship. Also requires 0–2 years of experience. Familiar with standard concepts, practices, and procedures within a particular field. Relies on limited experience and judgment to plan and accomplish goals. Performs a variety of tasks. Typically reports to a supervisor/manager.

A typical Audiologist earns a median base salary of $49,986.

Audiologist

25th percentile	Median	75th percentile
$45,488	$49,986	$55,964

Electrician I (Construction and Installation)

Inspects, repairs, installs, modifies, and maintains electrical/electronic systems, circuits, and equipment. Requires a high school diploma or its equivalent with 0–2 years of experience in the field or in a related area. May have to complete an apprenticeship and/or formal training in area of specialty. Has knowledge of commonly used concepts, practices, and procedures within a particular field. Relies on instructions and pre-established guidelines to perform the functions of the job. Works under immediate supervision. Primary job functions do not typically require exercising independent judgment. Typically reports to a supervisor/manager.

A typical Electrician I earns a median base salary of $31,862.

Electrician I

25th percentile	Median	75th percentile
$27,710	$31,862	$37,014

Graphic Design Specialist (Printing and Publishing)

Uses computer graphic systems to produce graphic sketches, designs, and copy layouts. May require an associate's degree or its equivalent and 2–4 years of experience in the field or in a related area. Familiar with standard concepts, practices, and procedures within a particular field. Relies on limited experience and judgment to plan and accomplish goals. Performs a variety of tasks. Works under general supervision; typically reports to a supervisor or manager. A great deal of creativity and latitude is expected.

A typical Graphic Design Specialist earns a median base salary of $39,446.

Graphic Design Specialist

25th percentile	Median	75th percentile
$35,241	$39,446	$44,540

Astronomer (Science and Research)

Studies, researches, and analyzes celestial phenomena. Develops methodologies to solve problems in physics and mathematics. May require an advanced degree and at least 2–4 years of direct experience in the field. A Ph.D. is required for research and development positions. Familiar with a variety of the field's concepts, practices, and procedures. Relies on limited experiences and judgment to plan and accomplish goals. Performs a variety of tasks. A wide degree of creativity and latitude is expected.

A typical Astronomer earns a median base salary of $80,447.

Astronomer

25th percentile	Median	75th percentile
$79,168	$80,447	$92,826

Pharmacist (Healthcare — Practitioners)

Under the direction of a physician, compounds and dispenses prescribed drug. Requires a bachelor's degree and/or an advanced degree in pharmacy and is licensed to practice. Familiar with standard concepts, practices, and procedures within a particular field. Relies on experience and judgment to plan and accomplish goals. Performs a variety of tasks. Typically reports to a manager or supervisor. A certain degree of creativity and latitude is required.

A typical Pharmacist earns a median base salary of $67,628.

Pharmacist

25th percentile	Median	75th percentile
$64,381	$67,628	$72,086

Plumber I (Construction and Installation)

Inspects, repairs, installs, modifies, and maintains plumbing fixtures in heating, water and drainage systems. May require a high school diploma or its equivalent with 0–2 years of experience in the field or in a related area. May be required to meet certain certifications in plumbing. Has knowledge of commonly used concepts, practices, and procedures within a particular field. Relies on instructions and pre-established guidelines to perform the functions of the job. Works under immediate supervision. Primary job functions do not typically require exercising independent judgment. Typically reports to a supervisor/manager.

A typical Plumber I earns a median base salary of $29,296.

Plumber I

25th percentile	Median	75th percentile
$25,435	$29,296	$36,610

Teacher, Elementary School (Education)

Prepares lesson plans and instructs children. Evaluates and monitors student's performance. Requires a bachelor's degree and 2–4 years of experience in the field or in a related area. Some states require that teachers be certified. Familiar with standard concepts, practices, and procedures within a particular field. Relies on limited experience and judgment to plan and accomplish goals. Performs a variety of tasks. Works under general supervision; typically reports to the principal. A certain degree of creativity and latitude is required. Note: Median base salary figures represent teachers with 15 years of experience.

A typical Elementary Teacher School earns a median base salary of $42,811.

Elementary School Teacher

25th percentile	Median	75th percentile
$35,069	$42,811	$50,777

Landscape Architect
(Construction and Installation)

Plans and designs land areas for such projects as parks and other recreational facilities, airports, highways, hospitals, schools, land subdivisions; and commercial, industrial, and residential sites. Requires a bachelor's degree in a related area and at least 4 years of experience in the field or in a related area. Familiar with a variety of the field's concepts, practices, and procedures. Relies on experience and judgment to plan and accomplish goals. Performs a variety of complicated tasks. May direct and lead the work of others. Typically reports to a manager or head of a unit/ department. A wide degree of creativity and latitude is expected.

A typical Landscape Architect earns a median base salary of $46,762.

Landscape Architect

25th percentile	Median	75th percentile
$38,305	$46,762	$56,150

For other job descriptions go to page 116.

"Odds On You" Revisited

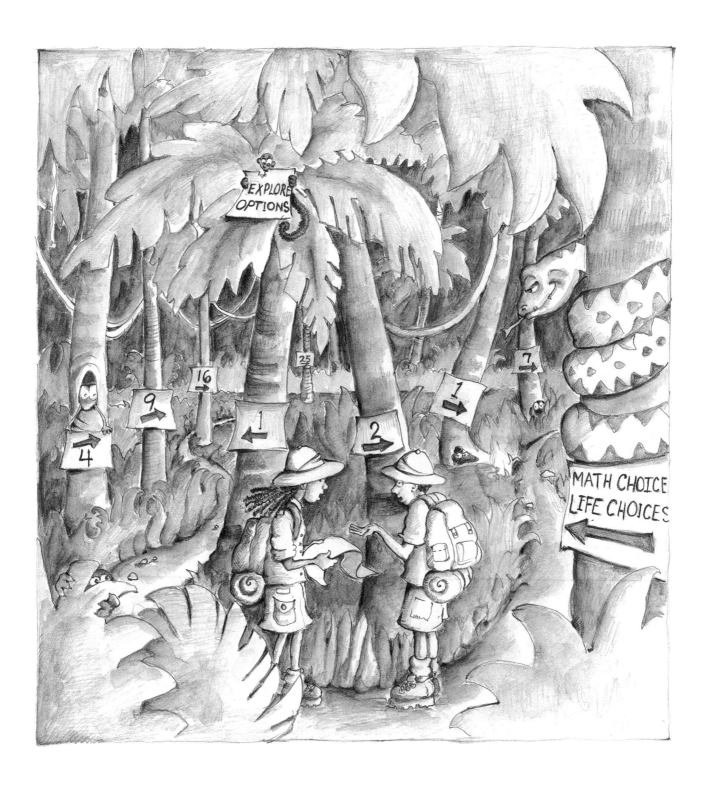

MATH AND CAREER OPTIONS

Why is this important?

Did you know that taking an additional algebra or geometry course might increase a person's lifetime earnings by 6% or more? The impact of an additional calculus course can be double that. As you can see, the effect of higher math courses on your child's future earnings is quite amazing.

In this activity, your family will play a statistical game that predicts your child's future, beginning at birth and ending when your child begins a career.

Julian and his dad are discussing classes for next year. Julian already completed the two math courses required to graduate from high school but had to work hard to get a C in both. He is now thinking about going to college and has met with his high school counselor. With college in mind, the counselor suggested that Julian and his family play the following simulation. Let's help them discover what might lie ahead for students like Julian.

How

- Two or more people can play this game.

- Using the "Odds On You" Game Board on page 54, begin with Set 1 by rolling a die to determine your gender. Follow the directions on the game board.

- As you roll, record your results on the This Could Be Your Life Worksheet on page 61.

- Continue rolling the dice until you complete the game.

- Be sure to complete Set 4. Are you satisfied with how chance decided your child's fate?

- Talk about how math courses affect your child's future career options. Were there any surprises in your results?

- For more information on careers, review the Highlighted Job Descriptions and Salaries on page 116.

MATERIALS

pencil or pen

scratch paper

dice

"Odds On You" Revisited
  Game Board, page 53

This Could Be Your Life
  Worksheet, page 61

Here's More...

Talk with your child's school counselor about:
1. Your family's goals for your child.
2. How your child is doing in math.
3. What math courses, resources, and support your child needs to accomplish the desired goals.

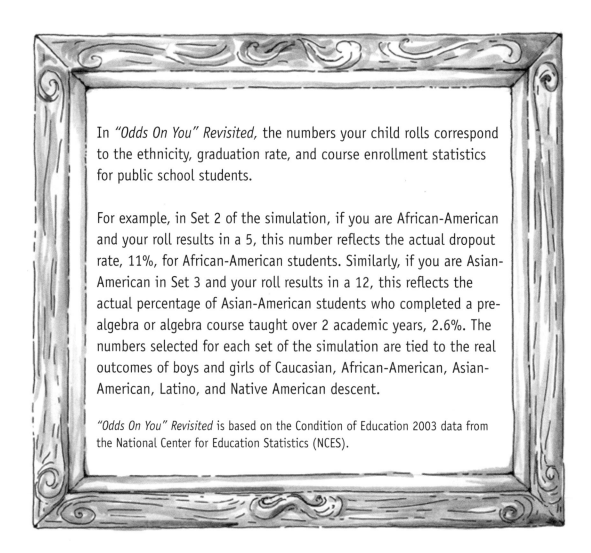

In *"Odds On You" Revisited,* the numbers your child rolls correspond to the ethnicity, graduation rate, and course enrollment statistics for public school students.

For example, in Set 2 of the simulation, if you are African-American and your roll results in a 5, this number reflects the actual dropout rate, 11%, for African-American students. Similarly, if you are Asian-American in Set 3 and your roll results in a 12, this reflects the actual percentage of Asian-American students who completed a pre-algebra or algebra course taught over 2 academic years, 2.6%. The numbers selected for each set of the simulation are tied to the real outcomes of boys and girls of Caucasian, African-American, Asian-American, Latino, and Native American descent.

"Odds On You" Revisited is based on the Condition of Education 2003 data from the National Center for Education Statistics (NCES).

"Odds on You" Revisited GAME BOARD set 1

ROLL

GENDER

1 ▸ 1 die

If the result is: 2, 4, 6 — You are a girl

If the result is: 1, 3, 5 — You are a boy

ETHNICITY

2 ▸ 2 dice and add numbers

If the result is: 2–8 or 12 — You are Caucasian

If the result is: 9–11 — *Roll again to determine your ethnicity.*

If the result is: 3, 7, 9–11 — You are African-American

If the result is: 4 — You are Asian-American

If the result is: 5, 6, 8,12 — You are Latina or Latino.

If the result is: 2 — You are Native American.

3 ▸ Write who you are on your *This Could Be Your Life Worksheet.* For example, I am a Latina girl.

4 ▸ Go to **Set 2.**

"Odds on You" Revisited GAME BOARD set 2

HIGH SCHOOL GRADUATE?

ROLL

1 If you are Caucasian:

2 dice and add numbers

If the result is: 2, 4–12 — You will graduate from high school.

If the result is: 3 — You dropped out of high school. **Go to Set 4.**

If you are African-American:

2 dice and add numbers

If the result is: 2–4, or 6–12 — You will graduate from high school.

If the result is: 5 — You dropped out of high school. **Go to Set 4.**

If you are Asian-American:

2 dice and add numbers

If the result is: 3–12 — You will graduate from high school.

If the result is: 2 — You dropped out of high school. **Go to Set 4.**

If you are Latino/a:

2 dice and add numbers

If the result is: 2–6, 8, 9, 11 — You will graduate from high school.

If the result is: 7, 10, 12 — You dropped out of high school. **Go to Set 4.**

If you are Native American:

2 dice and add numbers

If the result is: 2, 3, 5–9, 11, 12 — You will graduate from high school.

If the result is: 4, 10, — You dropped out of high school. **Go to Set 4.**

---

2 Write who you are on your *This Could Be Your Life Worksheet.*
For example, I am a Latino boy who graduated from high school.

3 Go to **Set 3.**

"Odds on You" Revisited GAME BOARD set 3

If you are Caucasian

1 ▶ ROLL 2 dice and add numbers

HIGH SCHOOL MATH COURSES

Course you enroll in:

If the result is: 2 → **Non-academic math**–Highest level completed was general or basic math.

If the result is: 3 → **Low-academic math**–Highest level completed was pre-algebra, algebra taught over 2 academic years, informal geometry.

MIDDLE-ACADEMIC MATH

If the result is: 2, 3, 4, 5, 6 → **Middle-academic math**–Highest level completed was algebra I, plane & solid geometry, unified math I & II, pure math.

If the result is: 7, 8, 9, 10, 11, 12 → **Middle-academic math**–Highest level completed was algebra II, unified math III.

If the result is: 4, 5, 6, 10, 11 [**Roll again**]

ADVANCED-ACADEMIC MATH

If the result is: 2, 4, 5, 6 → **Advanced academic math**–Highest level completed was algebra III, algebra/trigonometry/analytical geometry, linear algebra, probability/ statistics.

If the result is: 7, 8, 11 → **Advanced academic math**–Highest level completed was pre-calculus or introduction to analysis.

If the result is: 3, 9, 10, 12 → **Advanced academic math**–Highest level completed was: Advanced Placement (AP) calculus; calculus; or calculus/analytical geometry.

If the result is: 7, 8, 9, 12 [**Roll again**]

2 ▶ Write who you are on your *This Could Be Your Life Worksheet.* For example, I am a Caucasian girl who graduated from high school, and the highest-level math course I completed was Algebra II.

3 ▶ Go to **Set 4.**

"Odds on You" Revisited GAME BOARD `set 3`

HIGH SCHOOL MATH COURSES

If you are African-American

1 **ROLL** 2 dice and add numbers

Course you enroll in:

If the result is: 2, 12 → **Non-academic math**–Highest level completed was general or basic math.

If the result is: 4 → **Low-academic math**–Highest level completed was pre-algebra, algebra taught over 2 academic years, informal geometry.

MIDDLE-ACADEMIC MATH

If the result is: 2, 3, 4, 5, 6, 12 → **Middle-academic math**–Highest level completed was algebra 1, plane & solid geometry, unified math I & II, pure math.

If the result is: 7, 8, 9, 10, 11 → **Middle-academic math**–Highest level completed was algebra II, unified math III.

If the result is: 7, 8, 9, 10, 11 — **Roll again**

ADVANCED-ACADEMIC MATH

If the result is: 2, 3, 4, 5, 6, 12 → **Advanced academic math**–Highest level completed was algebra III, algebra/trigonometry/analytical geometry, linear algebra, probability/ statistics.

If the result is: 8, 9, 11 → **Advanced academic math**–Highest level completed was pre-calculus or introduction to analysis.

If the result is: 7, 10 → **Advanced academic math**–Highest level completed was: Advanced Placement (AP) calculus; calculus; or calculus/analytical geometry.

If the result is: 3, 5, 6 — **Roll again**

2 Write who you are on your *This Could Be Your Life Worksheet*. For example, I am an African-American boy who graduated from high school, and the highest-level math course I completed was Algebra II. ▶ Go to **Set 4.**

"Odds on You" Revisited GAME BOARD
set 3

If you are Asian-American

1 ▶ **ROLL** 2 dice and add numbers

Course you enroll in:

Non-academic math–Highest level completed was general or basic math.

If the result is: 2

Low-academic math–Highest level completed was pre-algebra, algebra taught over 2 academic years, informal geometry.

If the result is: 12

MIDDLE-ACADEMIC MATH

Middle-academic math–Highest level completed was algebra I, plane & solid geometry, unified math I & II, pure math.

If the result is: 2, 3, 4, 5, 6

Middle-academic math–Highest level completed was algebra II, unified math III.

If the result is: 7, 8, 9, 10, 11, 12

If the result is: 3, 4, 5, 6   **Roll again**

ADVANCED-ACADEMIC MATH

Advanced academic math–Highest level completed was algebra III, algebra/trigonometry/analytical geometry, linear algebra, probability/ statistics.

If the result is: 9, 10,

Advanced academic math–Highest level completed was pre-calculus or introduction to analysis.

If the result is: 2, 3, 4, 5, 6, 12

Advanced academic math–Highest level completed was: Advanced Placement (AP) calculus; calculus; or calculus/analytical geometry.

If the result is: 7, 8, 11

If the result is: 7, 8, 9, 10, 11   **Roll again**

2 ▶ Write who you are on your *This Could Be Your Life Worksheet.* For example, I am an Asian-American girl who graduated from high school, and the highest-level math course I completed was Algebra II.

3 ▶ Go to **Set 4.**

"Odds on You" Revisited GAME BOARD set 3

1 **ROLL** 2 dice and add numbers

HIGH SCHOOL MATH COURSES

If you are **Latino**

Course you enroll in:

If the result is: 2, 3 → **Non-academic math**–Highest level completed was general or basic math.

If the result is: 4 → **Low-academic math**–Highest level completed was pre-algebra, algebra taught over 2 academic years, informal geometry.

MIDDLE-ACADEMIC MATH

If the result is: 3, 4, 5, 9, 10, 11, 12 → **Middle-academic math**–Highest level completed was algebra I, plane & solid geometry, unified math I & II, pure math.

If the result is: 2, 6, 7, 8 → **Middle-academic math**–Highest level completed was algebra II, unified math III.

If the result is: 7, 8, 9, 10, 11, 12 — **Roll again**

ADVANCED-ACADEMIC MATH

If the result is: 8, 9, 11 → **Advanced academic math**–Highest level completed was algebra III, algebra/trigonometry/analytical geometry, linear algebra, probability/ statistics.

If the result is: 2, 3, 4, 5, 6 → **Advanced academic math**–Highest level completed was pre-calculus or introduction to analysis.

If the result is: 7, 10, 12 → **Advanced academic math**–Highest level completed was: Advanced Placement (AP) calculus; calculus; or calculus/analytical geometry.

If the result is: 5, 6 — **Roll again**

2 Write who you are on your *This Could Be Your Life Worksheet*. For example, I am a Latino boy who graduated from high school, and the highest-level math course I completed was Algebra II.

3 ▶ Go to **Set 4.**

"Odds on You" Revisited GAME BOARD

set 3

1 ▶ **ROLL** 2 dice and add numbers

If you are Native American

Course you enroll in:

If the result is: 2, 4 ———▶ **Non-academic math**–Highest level completed was general or basic math.

If the result is: 3 ———▶ **Low-academic math**–Highest level completed was pre-algebra, algebra taught over 2 academic years, informal geometry.

MIDDLE-ACADEMIC MATH

If the result is: 2, 6, 7, 8, ———▶ **Middle-academic math**–Highest level completed was algebra I, plane & solid geometry, unified math I & II, pure math.

If the result is: 3, 4, 5, 9, 10, 11, 12 ———▶ **Middle-academic math**–Highest level completed was algebra II, unified math III.

If the result is: 7, 8, 9, 10, 11, 12 **Roll again**

ADVANCED-ACADEMIC MATH

If the result is: 2, 4, 5, 6 ———▶ **Advanced academic math**–Highest level completed was algebra III, algebra/trigonometry/analytical geometry, linear algebra, probability/ statistics.

If the result is: 3, 7, 10, 11, 12 ———▶ **Advanced academic math**–Highest level completed was pre-calculus or introduction to analysis.

If the result is: 5, 6 **Roll again**

If the result is: 8, 9 ———▶ **Advanced academic math**–Highest level completed was: Advanced Placement (AP) calculus; calculus; or calculus/analytical geometry.

HIGH SCHOOL MATH COURSES

2 ▶ Write who you are on your *This Could Be Your Life Worksheet*. For example, I am a Native American girl who graduated from high school, and the highest-level math course I completed was Algebra II. **3** ▶ Go to **Set 4.**

"Odds on You" Revisited GAME BOARD

Proceed directly to the **Career Options Chart** on page 43 to find the jobs that you are academically prepared to pursue.

Record these job titles on the *This Could Be Your Life Worksheet.*

Now play again.

Did you drop out of high school? If so, write down what you think your career options might be. Discuss these with your family.

Now play two more times.

Remember, **"Odds On You" Revisited** is a simulation. You and your child can determine high school graduation and math course enrollment.

This Could be Your Life WORKSHEET

As you roll, use this page to record your dice rolls and results.

Set 1: Who am I?

Gender dice roll:_____ Ethnicity dice roll: _____

Write who you are below. For example, I am a Latino boy.

_____

Set 2: Will I graduate from high school?

Graduation dice roll:_____

Now write who you are below. For example, I am a Latino boy who will graduate from high school or I am a Latino boy who dropped out of high school.

_____

_____

Set 3: What math courses will I take?

1st Math course roll:_____2nd Math course roll: _____

Write the math courses you completed below.

_____

_____

Set 4: What career options do I have?

Proceed directly to the Career Options Chart on page 43 to find the jobs that you are academically prepared to pursue. Record these job titles below. Now play again.

_____

_____

Did you drop out of high school? If so, write down what you think your career options might be. Discuss these with your family. Now play two more times.

_____

_____

Remember, *"Odds On You"* Revisited is a simulation. You and your child can determine high school graduation and math course enrollment. Review the Highlighted Job Descriptions and Salaries starting on page 116 for more career information.

Putting the PSAT Together.
Is Your Child College Bound?

MATERIALS

Puzzle, page 64

scissors

pencils

paper

PSAT Puzzle Chart,
   page 65

The National Merit Scholarship Corporation, a nonprofit group created in 1955, sponsors one of the nation's most prestigious academic competitions. It sponsors more than $30 million annually in privately funded scholarships to college-bound students.

Each year, 16,000 top-scoring public and private school students become semifinalists. To ensure geographic diversity, the number of semifinalists in each state is based on its share of the national population of graduating high school seniors.

Why is this important?

It is our belief that all children should be academically prepared to attend college. Some students may choose to enter college directly after high school. Others may choose to attend college later in life. Whenever one decides to go, preparing for college can be puzzling. As with most educational decisions, it is best to know all the facts earlier rather than later.

College prep exams are tests that colleges and universities use to help decide student admissions. The exams are one of several factors used by colleges to gauge if a student will be successful.

The Preliminary Scholastic Aptitude Test/National Merit Scholarship Qualifying Test (PSAT/NMQT) is taken before the Scholastic Aptitude Test (SAT). The PSAT gives an indication of how students will score on the SAT. It also allows students to qualify for National Merit Scholarships. Although the PSAT is not required for college admissions, it is recommended that high school students take this test.

In the following activity, you will assemble a puzzle that contains information about the PSAT exam.

How

• Make a copy of the PSAT Puzzle on page 64, and cut out the pieces.

• Work with your child to assemble the puzzle.

• Read the information on each piece with your child.

• Discuss the information. Did you and your child discover any surprises in the information?

• Make notes from your discussion on the PSAT Puzzle Chart on page 65.

• Talk with your child's math teacher about the PSAT test. Tell the teacher that your child is planning on taking the PSAT in high school, and ask for suggestions on ways to prepare your child.

Here's More...

• Now do the SAT Puzzle activity on pages 66–69.

• To find out when the test is given in your area, contact:

The College Board
45 Columbus Avenue
NY, NY 10023-6992
212.713.8000

or online at
www.collegeboard.com

The College Board website has valuable information including:
• online registration for PSAT and SAT tests,
• relatively inexpensive test prep materials,
• suggestions for paying for college.

PSAT PUZZLE

What is the maximum time allowed to take the PSAT?

Two hours and 10 minutes.

Math content

Students should have a basic knowledge of arithmetic, algebra, and geometry.

How do students receive their scores?

Score reports are mailed to high school principals in December. For homeschoolers, scores are sent directly to the home address.

What does PSAT stand for?

Preliminary Scholastic Aptitude Test

Purpose

Provides practice for the SAT and SAT II. Also gives students a chance to qualify for the National Merit Scholarship Corporation's programs.

When should students take this test?

They should take it in the junior year of high school. It can be taken earlier, but it is a junior level test so scores may be low if taken before the junior year.

Scoring

There are three sections in the test: critical reading, math, and writing. Possible scores range from 20 to 80 for each section. The average section score for juniors is 49.

What calculators can a student use?

A student may use almost any scientific or graphing calculator on Math Level IC and Level IIC.

Format

PSAT is "speeded" by design. This means that many test takers are unable to finish all the questions in the time allowed.

Scoring

Student Produced Responses: When a student writes in the answers, each correct answer = 1 point. No points are given for an incorrect answer. **Multiple Choice Answered Correctly:** Students receive 1 point for each correct answer. Multiple Choice Answered Incorrectly: Subtract 1/3 point for each 4-choice question. Subtract 1/4 point for each 5-choice question.

Content

Measures critical reading, math problem solving, and writing skills.

Math format

Two 25-minute math sections with a total of 38 math questions. Twenty of the questions are regular multiple-choice, and 10 are student-produced responses.

What purpose does the PSAT serve?

What's the content on the test?

What's the format?

How is it scored?

Other notes:

Putting the SAT Puzzle Together. Is Your Child College Bound?

MATERIALS

Puzzle, page 68

scissors

pencils

paper

SAT Puzzle Chart, page 69

What is the SAT II?
The SAT II is a one-hour multiple choice test in a specific subject such as U.S. history, French, modern Hebrew, biology, literature, and math. There are two levels of math tests. Level IC is intended for students who have completed Algebra I, Algebra II, and geometry. Level IIC is intended for students who have taken Level IC requirements, pre-calculus and trigonometry.

We recommend that you do Putting the PSAT Together _activity on page 62 before beginning this one._

Why is this important?

It is our belief that all children should be academically prepared to attend college. Your child may decide to enter college directly after high school or attend later in life. Whenever she decides to go, preparing for college can be puzzling.

The Scholastic Aptitude Test (SAT) is one of several factors used by colleges to gauge if a student will be successful. SAT scores are required for admission to the majority of colleges and universities in the country.

As with most educational decisions, it is best for families to know all the facts earlier rather than later. Timing is everything. An important piece to the SAT puzzle is knowing its purpose, format, and the content that it covers. This information can maximize a student's performance.

In the following activity, you will assemble a puzzle that contains information about the SAT exam.

How

- Make a copy of the SAT puzzle on page 68, and cut out the pieces.

- Work with your child to assemble the puzzle.

- Read the information on each piece with your child.

- Discuss the information. What new information did you and your child discover?

- Make notes from your discussion on the SAT Puzzle Chart on page 69.

- Talk with your child's math teacher about the SAT. Make sure the teacher knows that your child is planning on taking the SAT in high school, and ask for suggestions on ways to improve your child's performance.

Here's More...

• To find out when the test is given in your area, contact:
The College Board
45 Columbus Avenue
NY, NY 10023-6992
212.713.8000

or online at
www.collegeboard.com

The College Board website has valuable information including:
• online registration for PSAT and SAT tests,
• relatively inexpensive test prep materials,
• suggestions for paying for college.

SAT PUZZLE

Purpose of the SAT

Many colleges and universities use the SAT as one indicator of a student's readiness to do college-level work. Other considerations include class rank, high school GPA, extracurricular activities, personal essay, and teacher recommendations.

Sample question

Al, Sonja, and Carol are to divide **n** coins among themselves. If Sonja receives twice as many coins as Carol and if Al receives twice as many coins as Sonja, then how many coins does Carol receive, in terms of n?

(A) $\dfrac{n}{2}$　　(B) $\dfrac{n}{3}$　　(C) $\dfrac{n}{4}$　　(D) $\dfrac{n}{6}$　　(E) $\dfrac{n}{7}$

The answer is E or $\dfrac{n}{7}$

Format

There are three sections to the SAT: critical reading, mathematics, and writing. It is a three-hour-and-35-minute test.

Preparation

Studies show that good coaching courses can raise students' scores by 100 points or more.

Format

This SAT includes a new writing section consisting of a 25-minute essay to test writing ability and 35 minutes of multiple-choice questions to see how well students use standard written English.

Math format

Students are given 70 minutes to complete the math section. There are three sections—two 25-minute and one 20-minute.

Calculator use

Students may use almost any scientific or graphing calculator while taking the Math Level I-C and Level II-C tests.

Design

The SAT test is "speeded" by design. This means that some test takers will not be able to finish all the questions in the time allotted.

Scoring scale

All sections (verbal, math, and writing) are scored on a 200- to 800-point scale. Two sub scores are given for the writing section. The essay portion has a scale of 2–12 points, and the multiple choice has a scale of 20–80.

Math format

There are two types of math questions. There are multiple-choice questions with 5 possible responses. There are also questions where students write in the answers.

Math format

Students taking the SAT need three years of math including Algebra II. The SAT features expanded math topics such as exponential growth, absolute value, and functional notation, The test places greater emphasis on linear functions, manipulations with exponents, and properties of tangent lines.

What purpose does the SAT serve?

What is the math content on the SAT?

What is the format?

How is the SAT scored?

What are some of the ways to prepare my child for the SAT?

How does the test compare in format, preparations, etc., to other tests children have to take?

What is the SAT II test?

What questions do I still have about the SAT?

Here you will see the math concepts addressed, e.g., algebra and geometry.

SAMPLE MATH ACTIVITY PAGE

MATERIALS

graph paper
scratch paper
colored pencils
 or pens

This section includes a list of materials you will need for the activity.

Why is this important?

In this activity you will see how increasing the amount of butter will help you bake a certain number of chocolate chip cookies. When you know how much butter you have, you can figure out how many dozen cookies you can bake or vice versa. Seeing the relationship between numbers and their graphic display is important to success in algebra.

How

- Look at the table below. It tells you how many chocolate chip cookies you can make with a certain amount of butter.

  Amount of Butter   Chocolate Chip Cookies (in dozens)

- Talk together about the patterns you see.

- The **How** section gives step-by-step directions for doing the activity. The information is broken down into small pieces that are easy to follow and to comprehend. Examples that model the math your child will be learning are often provided.

- It is recommended that you make copies of coordinate grids, cards, dominoes, etc., as indicated. We suggest that you avoid writing in the book so that your family can revisit the activities.

- Take each activity at your child's pace.

- Asking your child questions throughout the activity will promote a deeper understanding of the math concepts.

- Encourage your child to talk about her thinking as she proceeds through the mathematics.

- Be patient and listen to your child's responses. If your child has difficulties, try not to give him the answers. Instead, ask questions that will help clarify any confusion that your child might have.

- Remember that you do not have to be a math expert to help your child.

This section describes how the mathematics in the activity contribute to your child's learning. Sometimes you will find out why middle school children have difficulty with a particular math concept. Sometimes you will read about careers that require algebra or geometry.

These instructions and questions extend and vary the activity.

Here's More. . .

- Hate to bake? The Sweet On You Bakery sells oatmeal raisin cookies at 3 for $1.00. Create a table that shows the cost for 3, 6, 9, 12, 15, and 18 cookies. Write the ordered pairs and plot them on the graph on page xx. Draw a line through the points to connect them. What does your line look like? How does it compare to your chocolate chip cookie graph?

The math activities in *The Journey—Through Middle School Math* were created as nonthreatening investigations for your family to explore. Enjoying math with your child can be full of discovery and excitement.

If your child's answers do not match the ones provided, make this an opportunity to use an effective problem-solving strategy—working backwards. Often, there will be several ways to achieve a correct answer. Work with your child to look at different approaches. The answers in this book are not meant to STOP your family's thinking but to stimulate it.

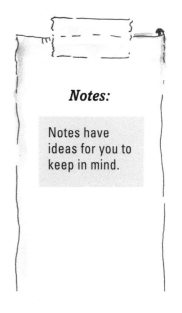

Notes:

Notes have ideas for you to keep in mind.

A variable is a letter or symbol used to represent an unknown number or quantity.

Sidebars provide additional math connections.

CHOCOLATE CHIP COOKIE GRAPHS

MATERIALS

Coordinate Grid Paper,
    page 124
scratch paper
colored pencils
    or pens

1 stick of butter
  (1 stick = 1 cup)
2 cups flour
1/2 T. sugar
1 t. baking powder
8 oz. chocolate chips

In a bowl, mix butter
and sugar......

Why is this important?

Children have been creating and graphing simple patterns since early elementary school. In middle school your child needs to understand the relationship between the data in a table and its pictorial representation on a graph.

Understanding the relationship between numbers and their graphic display is important to success in algebra and geometry. In this activity you will see how increasing the amount of butter will help you bake a certain number of chocolate chip cookies. When you know how much butter you have, you can figure out how many dozen cookies you can bake or vice versa.

How

- Look at the table below. It tells you how many chocolate chip cookies you can make with a certain amount of butter.

- Work with a partner, and talk together about the patterns you see.

- Once you have discovered a pattern, complete the table below. How many cookies could you make with 7 cups of butter? 8 or 9 cups? How do you know?

- In order to place (plot) the numbers on a graph, we need to make "ordered pairs." Our ordered pairs come from listing first the amount of butter, then the number of cookies (in dozens).

- Complete the Ordered Pairs column in the table below.

Graphing the pattern

Amount of Butter	Chocolate Chip Cookies (in dozens)	Ordered Pairs
1 cup	2	(1, 2)
2 cups	4	(2, 4)
3 cups	6	
⋮		

CHOCOLATE CHIP COOKIE GRAPHS

Often students do not know which number in the ordered pair to move along the x-axis (horizontal) or the y-axis (vertical). In this activity, asking them to move over and up is a nice way to describe what to do.

It is also important to know that the coordinate plane is divided into 4 quadrants. All of the points plotted in this activity have been in quadrant 1, because no numbers less than zero appear in the table.

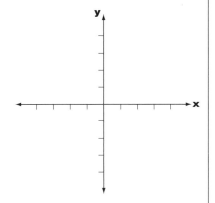

• Now make a graphic display of your pattern. Use the grid paper on page 124 to plot the ordered pairs. The first number tells you how many to go over along the x-axis, and the second number tells you how far to go along the y-axis.

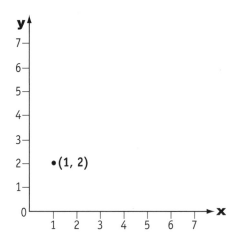

• Talk with your partner or family members about the information on the graph.

• What's the relationship between the amount of butter and the number of chocolate chip cookies?

• What do you think are the benefits of using a table? A graph? An equation?

Here's More. . .

• Hate to bake? The Sweet On You Bakery sells oatmeal raisin cookies at 3 for $1.00. Create a table that shows the cost for 3, 6, 9, 12, 15, and 18 cookies. Write the ordered pairs, and plot them on the graph paper. What does your graph look like? How does it compare to your chocolate chip cookie graph?

• The bakery at the Food Friendly Supermarket sells brownies at 3 for 75 cents. Create a table that shows the cost for 2, 4, 5, 8, 10, 12, 15, and 18 brownies. Write the ordered pairs and plot them on the same graph as the Sweet On You Bakery. Note that it might be a good idea to plot these points with a different color pen or pencil.

• Ask your child to describe the two graphs. Does one look steeper than the other? Do they intersect or cross at any point? If you want to buy dessert for 12 friends, what would you buy and why? Which graph represents the better buy?

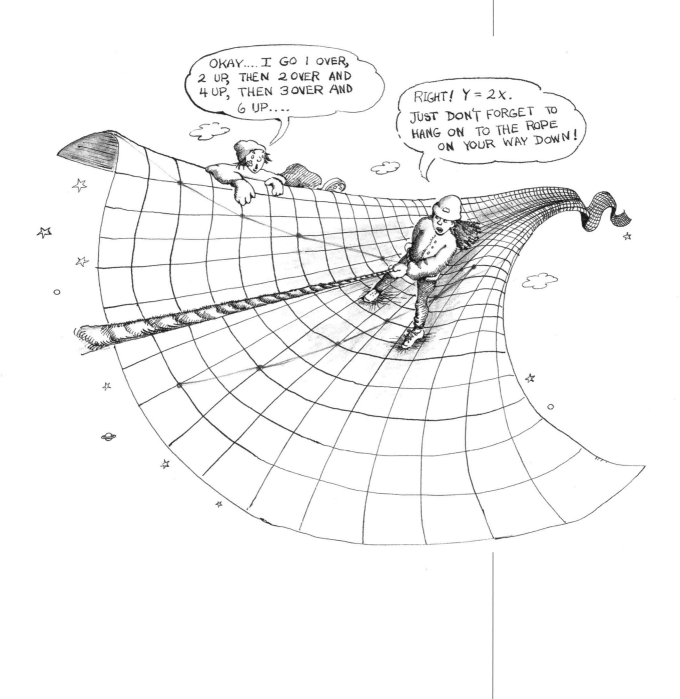

ADJACENT TRIANGLES

Why is this important?

Recognizing and generalizing patterns is important in all of mathematics and its applications. When we "generalize" a pattern, we come up with a rule we can use to find the outcome for every situation in that pattern. The ability to generalize a pattern and fill in a table or chart is a powerful step towards understanding equations and graphs in algebra. In this activity, you will create new shapes using triangles and investigate how the perimeters of these shapes change.

MATERIALS
paper
markers or pencils
Triangle Grid Paper,
    page 126
Square Grid Paper,
    page125

How

- The distance around a shape is called the perimeter. We use the term "equilateral" to indicate that all sides of a shape are the same length. The shape below is an equilateral triangle because each of its sides has a length of 2 units. Label the length of each side.

- How can you find the perimeter of this triangle? (You can add the lengths of the 3 sides or multiply the length of one side by 3.) What is the perimeter?

- Suppose you want to retile your bathroom using tiles shaped like equilateral triangles. Draw two equilateral triangles with side lengths of 2 units and make sure that your triangles share at least one full side.

- Does your drawing look like one of the models below?

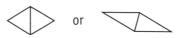

- What is the perimeter of the shape formed by 2 adjacent triangles?

- Lay out a sequence of shapes using 1, 2, 3, 4, 5, and 6 equilateral triangles, with side lengths of 2 units each. Make sure that each new triangle is adjacent to only 1 other triangle.

- Record the number of triangles and the perimeter of each new shape in the table below. Remember that the length of each side is 2 units.

Number of Adjacent Equilateral Triangles	Perimeter in Units
1	6
2	8
3	
4	
5	
6	

- Discuss the data with your children. What patterns do you see? Use words or sketches to describe your patterns.

- What would the perimeter be of 10 adjacent equilateral triangles? How do you know?

- Ask your child to generalize the pattern she sees by describing what happens to the perimeter as the number of triangles changes.

- Why doesn't the perimeter double, triple, or quadruple as you use 2, 3, or 4 triangles?

Here's More. . .

- Try the same problem using squares. Use the square grid paper on page 125. Assign the same length to each side and make sure that each new square shares a side with the one next to it.

- In a table, record the number of adjacent squares and the resulting perimeters.

- Is the pattern the same as the one with triangles or different? Why?

- Ask your child to generalize a pattern using the sequence of squares.

Children frequently look for patterns down one column of a table instead of across the columns. This can cause problems later when they have to write an equation that describes a pattern. In this activity, we want children to describe the relationship between the change in perimeter and the change in the number of triangles.

COUNTING THE GOOD TIMES

MATERIALS

50 beans or buttons

scratch paper or Post-its

pen or pencil

Why is this important?

Visualizing and modeling algebra problems are essential skills for middle-school students. These skills are especially critical for success in upper level mathematics and science courses. In this activity we will use beans or buttons to solve algebra problems based on written clues.

Adriane and Janelle are volunteering at the Good Times Record Store. The girls are completing their school community service requirements. Adriane and Janelle are making packages of CDs for senior citizens. Each CD package has no more than 50 CDs. Each package has a different combination of music types based on clue cards.

However, the girls are having trouble understanding how to solve the clue cards.

A prime number is a whole number greater than zero that has only two factors, one and itself.

An exponent tells you how many times a number is multiplied by itself or that it is raised to a certain power. For example,

Exponent

$3^{②} = 3 \times 3; \; 3^4 = 3 \times 3 \times 3 \times 3 = 81$

Base Number

Be careful, don't multiply the exponent and the base number as in the following example.

$3^2 \neq 3 \times 2 \qquad 3^2 \neq 6$

instead $3^2 = 3 \times 3 = 9$

A square number is the result of a number multiplied by itself. It is also called a figurate number because it can be represented by a geometric figure or arrangement. In this case the figure looks like a square. The illustrations below show why the figurate numbers 4 and 9 are called square numbers.

$9 = 3 \times 3 = 3^2$

$4 = 2 \times 2 = 2^2$

A multiple of a number can be found by skip counting on a number line. For example, to find multiples of 3, start at 3 and jump to every third number.

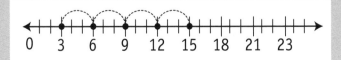

How

• Work with a family member. Use buttons or beans to help Adriane and Janelle solve the following clue card.

> **Berkeley Senior Center CD Package**
>
> 1. Three times the number of classical CDs as rock CDs
> 2. R&B CDs equal the number of classical CDs
> 3. Four times the number of jazz CDs as R&B CDs
> 4. The total number of CDs is 38

• The first clue shows that there are three times the number of classical CDs as rock. If you have 1 rock CD, how many classical CDs will you have? 2 rock CDs? 3 rock CDs?

Chart for Clue #1

Rock	Classical
1 bean	3 beans
2 beans	6 beans
3 beans	9 beans

• Clue # 2 says that you always have the same number of R&B CDs as classical. Looking back at the Chart for Clue #1, how many classical CDs did you have when you had 1 rock? So how many R&B CDs would you have? Does your answer agree with the Chart for Clue #2?

Chart for Clue #2

Rock	Classical	R & B	Jazz	Total
1 bean	3 beans	3 beans		
2 beans	6 beans	6 beans		
3 beans	9 beans	9 beans		

- The third clue tells you that there are four times the number of jazz as R&B CDs. Therefore, if you have 3 R&B CDs, you would multiply to find the number of jazz CDs: 3 X 4 = 12 jazz CDs. What if you have 6 R&B CDs? Do you see your answers in the Chart for Clue #3?

Chart for Clue #3

Rock	Classical	R & B	Jazz	Total
1 bean	3 beans	3 beans	12 beans	
2 beans	6 beans	6 beans	24 beans	
3 beans	9 beans	9 beans	36 beans	

- The fourth clue tells you that there are exactly 38 CDs in the Berkeley Senior Center CD Package. Now fill in the totals. Looking at the Chart for Clue #3, which combination fits this clue?

- Does the combination you selected fit all the clues? How do you know?

- Now help Adriane and Janelle solve the remaining CD packages. Do this with a partner. Remember: Sets have no more than 50 CDs. Some packages may have more than one solution. You can only package whole CDs.

Benjamin Banneker Home CD Package

1. Four times as many classical CDs as rock CDs
2. Three more R&B CDs than rock CDs
3. Two more jazz CDs than R&B CDs
4. The number of rock CDs is an odd number between 1 and 7
5. The total is 29

Lake Merritt CD Package

1. Three more salsa CDs than jazz CDs
2. Rock is 4 more than the number of salsa CDs
3. R&B is 5 more than the number of rock CDs
4. Salsa is double the number of jazz CDs

Knowland Senior Center CD Package

1. There is an equal number of salsa CDs as rock CDs
2. Four times as many R&B CDs as rock CDs
3. One-half as many jazz CDs as R&B CDs
4. Each type is a multiple of 5

Tilden CD Package

1. Jazz is double the number of salsa CDs
2. Rock is one-third the number of jazz CDs
3. R&B is half the number of jazz CDs
4. The number of classical CDs in this package is equal to the number of jazz CDs

Midtown CD Package

1. Half as many salsa CDs as jazz CDs
2. Half as many jazz CDs as classical CDs
3. Double the number of rock CDs as classical CDs
4. The number of salsa CDs is a fourth of the number of classical CDs

Pardee Home CD Package

1. If you square the number of classical CDs, it equals the number of rock CDs
2. Classical CDs equals the number of salsa CDs squared
3. The number of R&B CDs is the only even prime number
4. The sum of salsa, rock, and classical CDs is 2 less than 2 dozen

El Sobrante Park CD Package

1. Classical CDs are 4 times the number of rock CDs
2. R&B is double the number of rock CDs
3. Jazz is one-fifth the sum of rock and classical CDs combined
4. There is the same number of rock CDs as jazz CDs

ZERO PAIRS

Why is this important?

Students often think that there are no numbers less than zero. Others think that numbers less than zero are fractions. If not corrected, these misconceptions can be problematic when students study algebra.

Children need to remember that integers are positive and negative whole numbers. Numbers to the right of zero on a number line, such as 1, 2, 3, are positive. Numbers to the left of zero on a number line are negative, such as –1, –2, –3.

Zero is also an integer, and it is neither positive nor negative. As you move to the right on a number line, the value of the numbers increases. As you move to the left, the value decreases.

If you don't see a symbol in front of a number (either + or –), you can assume it is positive. Negative numbers always need a negative (–) sign.

In this activity, you and your family will be adding positive and negative numbers to your bank account and looking at the resulting balances.

MATERIALS

30 red beans
30 black beans
paper bowl or plate
scratch paper and
  pencils

How

• Work with a partner or your family.

• We can model adding positive and negative integers using beans. Let's use red beans to represent negative quantities and black beans as positive quantities.

• Let's pretend we are overdrawn $4 in our checking account. We can write that as –4.

• Ask your child to put 4 red beans in the bowl to represent –4.

- Now let's suppose you deposit $4. That is adding a +4. Let's put 4 black beans in the bowl to represent +4.

- Now take out every pair of beans (one red and one black). Do you have any beans left in the bowl?

- Mathematically you added −4 and its opposite, +4. We can write what you modeled in an **equation** like this:

$$(-4) + (+4) = 0$$

- We can draw the model like this:

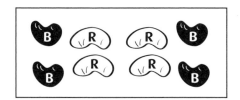

Anytime you add an integer and its opposite (like +4 and –4) you end up with zero. Numbers and their opposites are called zero pairs because their sum is zero. We say they "cancel each other out."

- What happens if you are overdrawn $8 and you deposit $8? Use the beans to model your account balance. Do you have any beans left over? How many zero pairs do you have?

- Suppose you are overdrawn $9 and deposit $15 to cover the overdraft. Using the beans, model what happens to your account balance. How many zero pairs do you have? How much money do you now have in your checking account?

- Let's draw what you discovered.

Now write the equation.

- Try the following with beans. Use the table below to record your bank account transactions.

Overdrawn	Deposit	Zero Pairs	Account Balance	Equation
–10	$13			
–12	$20			
–14	$29			

Here's More. . .

What would happen if you were overdrawn $35 and you deposited $21? Draw this transaction and write the equation for your bank balance now.

THE GAME OF KNOWN AND UNKNOWN

MATERIALS

20 beans or counters

10 paper squares, see
  Square Grid Paper, page
  125

pencil and paper

Leader Instructions,
  page 88

Leader Directional Cards
  A–E, pages 89–93

Algebraic Notations,
  page 94

A variable is a letter or symbol used to represent an unknown number or quantity.

Why is this important?

The transition between arithmetic and algebra is challenging for many children because algebra requires the ability to think abstractly. Using arithmetic rules and operations (+, −, ×, ÷) and applying them in algebra is essential to solving equations.

Variables are an important concept in algebra and one that children also have some difficulty understanding. Part of this difficulty is developmental. As children mature, their ability to reason or think abstractly increases. Another reason is a lack of experience working with variables.

In this activity, children use beans and paper squares to represent operations with numbers (known) and variables (unknown).

Vincent and his sister Vicky are always playing tricks on each other. Today Vicky brags, "I know a number trick. Without knowing what number you start with, I can tell you what number you end up with after a series of six steps." Vincent answers, "I bet you can't!"

The object of this game is to figure out Vicky's trick.

How

• Two people or several people can play this game together.

• Work with a partner or group and select a leader.

• Make a copy of the Leader Directional Cards on pages 89–94 and the paper squares on page 125. Cut out the paper squares.

• The leader sets up a partition around a handful of beans and the Leader Directional Cards so that no one else can see what she is doing.

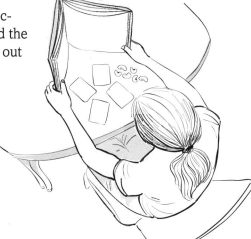

- The leader reads her own instructions on page 88.

- The leader then takes Card A and reads it to the group, step by step.

- Behind her partition, the leader uses beans and paper squares to model the instructions on Card A.

- At the same time, the group selects a secret number, follows the leader's directions, and records their process.

- After the six steps are read, the leader guesses the number the group has left.

- The same leader proceeds to Card B and repeats the process.

- Play again so that each person has a chance to be the leader for Cards A and B. Ask the group to select different numbers each time they play the game. Don't forget to review the Algebraic Notations for Cards A and B.

- See if you can explain how this game works. Discuss this with your partner or group.

- Proceed to Cards C through E, including the Algebraic Notations.

Here's More...
- After each person has an opportunity to be leader, here are some questions to talk about:

    1. Did it matter what the secret number was? Why or why not?

    2. How did using the beans and paper squares help you figure out what number you had left?

    3. In analyzing the steps, did you find any patterns?

    4. Can you explain Vicky's trick to your partner?

Leader Instructions

In this game, the paper squares represent variables in algebra. The beans represent a number or constant. Even though the secret number (variable) is unknown to the leader, she can still figure out the number the group has left.

Start with Card A on page 89. Remember that the leader needs to set up a partition so that no one else can see the Directional Cards. On a blank piece of paper, she makes her own model using beans and paper squares.

The leader reads the six steps one at a time to the group. At the same time, the leader follows the Card A model step by step and figures out the number the group has left. When the game is over, the same leader proceeds to Card B on page 90.

Play again so that each person has a chance to be the leader for Cards A and B. Make sure the group selects different secret numbers each time the game is played.

At the conclusion of Card B, each leader should be able to create her own models by making a drawing or using beans and paper squares. Review the Algebraic Notations for Cards A and B.

Then go ahead to Cards C through E. For these, the leader can draw her model on the blank cards on each page. The leader can also create her own model using beans and paper squares.

Ask your partner or the group to complete the Algebraic Notations for Cards C through E.

In mathematics, there are different types of constants. The type used in this activity is called an absolute constant. It is a particular number that never changes in value.

1. Select a secret number from 5 to 10.

 Represents group's secret number.

PAPER SQUARE

2. Add 5.

3. Multiply by 2.

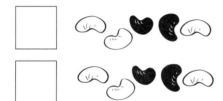

Note: *The direction is to multiply by 2, meaning you must double what you have including the secret number. One way to think of multiplication is as repeated addition.*

4. Subtract 4.

Note: *The direction is to subtract 4. Since the secret number is an unknown quantity, we can't subtract 4 from it. However, we can subtract 4 from the 10 beans.*

5. Divide by 2.

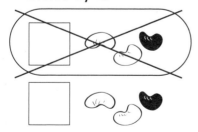

Note: *The direction is to divide by 2, meaning the total amount should be separated into two equal groups.*

6. Subtract your secret number.

Note: *Even though we don't know what the secret number is, we can take it away from the total.*

ANSWER: Leader tells the group: "You have 3 left."

1. Select a secret number from 20 to 30.

 Represents group's secret number.

PAPER SQUARE

2. Multiply by 4.

3. Add 8.

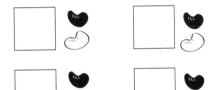

Note: *The direction is to add the quantity of 8, not add 8 secret numbers.*

4. Multiply by 2.

Note: *The direction is to multiply by 2. Although we don't know the quantity of the secret number we can represent "multiply by 2" by doubling the total amount of squares and beans.*

5. Divide by 8.

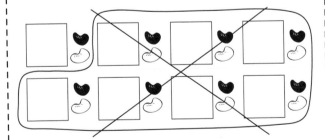

6. Subtract your secret number.

Note: *Even though we don't know what the secret number is we can subtract it easily from the total.*

ANSWER: Leader tells the group: "You have 2 left."

Leader Directional CARD

1. Select a secret number from 1 to 40.

[ ] Represents group's secret number.

PAPER SQUARE

2. Multiply by 3.

3. Add 12.

4. Divide by 3.

5. Subtract 2.

6. Subtract your secret number.

ANSWER: *Leader tells the group: "You have _____ left."*

1. Select a secret number from 50 to 100.

☐ Represents group's secret number.

PAPER SQUARE

2. Add 3.

3. Multiply by 3.

4. Subtract 9.

5. Divide by 3.

6. Subtract your secret number.

ANSWER: Leader tells the group: "You have _____ left."

1. Think of any whole number you want.

 Represents group's secret number.

PAPER SQUARE

2. Multiply by 4.

3. Add 8.

4. Multiply by 2.

5. Divide by 8.

6. Subtract your secret number.

ANSWER: Leader tells the group: "You have _____ left."

Algebraic Notation for Card A

1. Select a secret number from 5 to 10. **X**	2. Add 5. **X + 5**
3. Multiply by 2. **2(X + 5) = 2X + 10**	4. Subtract 4. **2X + 10 − 4 = 2X + 6**
5. Divide by 2. $$\frac{2X + 6}{2} = \frac{\overset{1}{2}X}{\underset{1}{2}} + \frac{\overset{3}{6}}{\underset{1}{2}} = X + 3$$	6. Subtract your secret number. **X + 3 − X** *Leader answer: You have 3 left X + 3 − X = 3*

Algebraic Notation for Card B

1. Select a secret number from 20 to 30. **X**	2. Multiply by 4. **X • 4 = 4X**
3. Add 8. **4X + 8**	4. Multiply by 2. **2(4X + 8) = 8X + 16**
5. Divide by 8. $$\frac{8X + 16}{8} = \frac{\overset{1}{8}X}{\underset{1}{8}} + \frac{\overset{2}{16}}{\underset{1}{8}} = X + 2$$	6. Subtract your secret number. **X + 2 − X** *Leader answer: You have 2 left X + 2 − X = 2*

Algebraic Notation for Card C

1. Select a secret number from 1 to 40.	2. Multiply by 3.
3. Add 12.	4. Divide by 3.
5. Subtract 2.	6. Subtract your secret number. *Leader answer: You have _____ left*

Algebraic Notation for Card D

1. Select a secret number from 50 to 100.	2. Add 3.
3. Multiply by 3.	4. Subtract 9.
5. Divide by 3.	6. Subtract your secret number. *Leader answer: You have _____ left*

Algebraic Notation for Card E

1. Think of any whole number you want.	2. Multiply by 4.
3. Add 8.	4. Multiply by 2.
5. Divide by 8.	6. Subtract your secret number. *Leader answer: You have _____ left*

DO I BELONG OR NOT?

Why is this important?

In arithmetic, students work with definite quantities such as 25 chairs or 200 dollars. In algebra, students begin to think abstractly and deal with the relationship of quantities to each other. Often these quantities or values are unknown.

Variables represent values that are unknown. For example, suppose the drama club is selling tickets to a play and the tickets are $7.00 each. The variable t can represent the unknown quantity of tickets. *7t* would then represent the total dollars in ticket sales.

Mathematicians call quantities such as *7t, d, –8,* and *xy²* "terms." Like or similar terms contain exactly the same variables raised to exactly the same powers. For example, *7t, –6t,* and *t* are like terms. They have the same variable *t* and each is raised to the first power. However, *4x* and *–7x²* are unlike terms. They have the same variable, x, but x is not raised to the same power in each term.

Being able to determine like terms is important when simplifying equations and expressions in algebra. In this activity, you will decide which are like terms and which are not.

MATERIALS
Do I Belong Cards, page 96
Do I Belong Record Sheet, page 96
pencil or pen

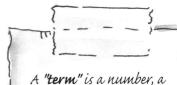

A *"term"* is a number, a variable, or a product of numbers and variables.

Remember that whenever you see terms such as b or xy, it means $1b^1$ or $1x^1y^1$; they are raised to the first power.

How

- Make a copy of the Do I Belong Cards on page 96, and cut them out.
- Talk to your partner about card #1. Discuss whether the terms on this card are like terms.
- Compare your answer with the answer given on the Record Sheet also on page 96.
- Continue discussing each card with your partner. Which are like terms and which are not?
- Record your thoughts for each card on the Record Sheet. Be sure to include why the terms are alike or different.

Here's More. . .

- Create your own set of cards with like and unlike terms.
- Try Let's Go To The Movies! on page 97.
- Try the Game of Term Dominoes on page 99.

Do I Belong CARDS

1.

b 7b

5.

−3x 14x 9y

9.

x^2 $5x^2$ $-12x^2$

2.

12y −3y

6.

−23x −4x −8x

10.

−5 8 −16

3.

18b 18c

7.

15t t 32s

11.

18w −23w $15w^2$

4.

$6a^2$ $-a^2$ $-23a^2$

8.

$7p^3$ $-p^3$ p^3

12.

y $21y^2$ −21x

Do I Belong Record Sheet

Which are like terms and which are not? Record your thoughts for each card below. Be sure to include why the terms are alike or different.

1. Like terms: same variable raised to the same power.	7.
2.	8.
3.	9.
4.	10.
5.	11.
6.	12.

LET'S GO TO THE MOVIES!

We recommend that you try Do I Belong or Not? *on page 95 before beginning this activity.*

Why is this important?

Like terms are important because they are used to simplify equations and expressions in algebra.

A term can be:
- a number
- a variable
- a combination of both such as *5x, –3a*, or *xy²*

Remember that whenever you see a term such as *x*, it means *x* is raised to the first power.

Like terms contain **exactly** the same variables raised to **exactly** the same powers. For example, *x²y, 3x²y* and *–5x²y* are like terms because they all have the same variables (x and y) and each variable is raised to the same power. In our example, the *x* in all three terms is raised to the second power and each *y* is raised to the first power.

In this activity, you and your partner will create 12 movie groups using like terms.

Preparation

Write each of the following algebraic terms on a piece of paper or index card.

a	$6a^2b$	$2xy^2$	–3	$5y^2$
$3b^2$	3	3a	$3a^2$	3b
$5yz^3$	–3b	–3a	b	a^2
y^2	xy	–5x	x^2	yz^3
$-3a^2$	$-4xy^2$	5x	$5x^2$	$-3b^2$
b^2	7xy	7	a^2b	x

MATERIALS
30 index cards or small
  pieces of paper
marking pens

$a^3 = a \times a \times a$
$a^3 \neq a \times 3$

Mr. Tsui and Ms. Diaz were discussing a whole school project for Martin Luther King Middle School. Century Hilltop Movie Theaters invited the entire school to preview 12 new kid-friendly movies. Mr. Tsui thought this would be a great opportunity to have students write movie reviews. Ms. Diaz thought it would be fun to sort students into movie review groups using like terms.

They decided to test their plan for sorting by using Ms. Diaz's class of 30 students.

Each student would receive a "movie ticket" with an algebraic term on it. Students would then be instructed to form 12 groups at the Century Theater Complex according to the like-term movie tickets.

How

- Work with a partner or family member.

- Shuffle the cards that you prepared earlier. These are your free movie tickets.

- With your partner, begin sorting the tickets into 12 like-term groups. For example, you and your partner can take one ticket each and compare them. Are your two tickets for the same movie? How do you know?

- Continue sorting the tickets. As you sort, discuss your findings. What did you discover about like terms? Does every movie have more than one person attending?

Here's More...

- Create enough new tickets so that there are five tickets for each movie group.

- Make up four new movie groups

THE GAME OF TERM DOMINOES

MATERIALS
Term Dominoes, page 102
paper
pencil or pen

You will find important mathematics information in Do I Belong or Not? *on page 95 and* Let's Go to The Movies! *on page 97 that will help you play this game. We suggest that you try these activities before beginning* The Game of Term Dominoes.

Why is this important?

Many children find combining like terms difficult. They don't understand that each variable represents a distinct quantity. For example, the variable **a** represents a different amount than the variable **b.** Simplifying equations and expressions in algebra depends on a child's ability to correctly combine like terms.

In this activity, you will play a game of strategy by matching like terms.

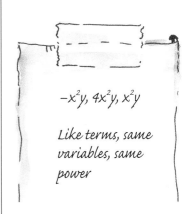

$-x^2y, 4x^2y, x^2y$

Like terms, same variables, same power

How

• Two people play this game. The object of this game is to get more points than your opponent.

• Make a copy of the Term Dominoes on page 102 and cut them out.

• Select one of the double term dominoes and place it face up between the two players. The first double domino is always placed horizontally. After that, any domino can be placed either horizontally or vertically.

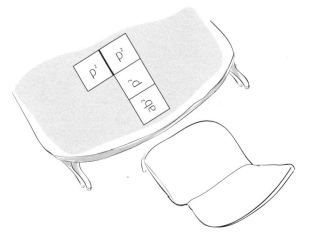

• Place all the remaining double and regular dominoes face down on the table and mix them up.

• Each player selects 5 dominoes. Take a peek at your dominoes, but don't allow your opponent to see them.

• Keep the remaining dominoes to use later.

• Decide which player will go first. Players will alternate turns.

• Try to make a match with the term on the double domino.

- If you cannot make a match, take a domino from the pile. If that one doesn't match, you lose your turn.

- Players alternate matching like terms until one player uses all her dominoes or the players can no longer make a match by using a domino from the pile.

- When a player uses all her dominoes, she declares "TD"–Term Domino and the games ends.

or

- If both players cannot make a match, the game ends.

Who wins?
- To determine who won the game, players calculate points.

- Points are calculated based on the dominoes remaining in a player's hand.

- Each player calculates her points by adding the exponents on her remaining dominoes. For example, y is worth one point, –y is worth one point, y^2 is worth two points, etc.

- Then each player exchanges points.

- The person with the most points wins the game.

- Play three times and see who wins the most games.

- Play a game cooperatively and discuss game strategy.

Here's More. . .
- Make up a different way to score points.

- Create more Term Dominoes.

$y = y^1$

y is raised to the first power.

Term **Dominoes**

p^2	p^2	y	y	$-a^2$	$-a^2$
$7x^4$	$7x^4$	ab^2	ab^2	9^3	9^3

y	p^2	$-a$	p^2	$-7x^4$	p^2
ab^2	p^2	9^3	p^2	$-a^2$	y
$7x^4$	y	ab^2	y	-9^3	y
$-7x^4$	$-a$	ab^2	a^2	9^3	$-ab^2$
ab^2	$-7x^4$	9^3	$7x^4$	9^3	$-ab^2$

MAKE YOUR GARDEN BIGGER

Why is this important?

Many practical problems have solutions based on similarity. Similarity is evident in many aspects of our everyday lives such as architecture, maps, and TV screens. The study of similarity is connected to ratio, proportion, and parallelism. Being able to determine whether a shape is similar to another is important in mathematics.

In this activity, you will change the lengths of various garden shapes and discuss how a new garden relates to the original.

MATERIALS

ruler with centimeter units
pencil
paper
calculator
Garden Shapes, page 106

In mathematics the word **similar** has a very specific meaning. Two shapes are said to be similar if they have the same angle measurement and the corresponding sides have the same ratio.

One way to determine similarity is by performing a ratio check. When corresponding sides of two or more shapes have the same ratio, then their angles will have the same measurement. The figures are said to be similar.

To perform a ratio check, let's compare the shortest to the longest side of the shape.

Triangle ABC
Ratio Check
shortest leg $\overline{CB}$ /longest leg $\overline{AB}$
2 cm /5 cm = 0.40

Triangle DEF
Ratio Check
shortest leg $\overline{FE}$ /longest leg $\overline{DE}$
5 cm /8 cm = 0.63

Triangle GHI
Ratio Check
shortest leg $\overline{IH}$ /longest leg $\overline{GH}$
6 cm /15 cm = 0.40

For example, if the length of side $\overline{CB}$ is 2 cm and the length of side $\overline{AB}$ is 5 cm, we write the ratio as 2/5 or 0.40.

Our ratio check is calculated by dividing the shortest leg (2 cm) by the longest leg (5 cm).

This ratio is not the same as the ratio of triangle ABC. Therefore, triangles DEF and ABC are not similar.

This third triangle has a ratio of 0.40, the same as triangle ABC. Therefore, the first and third triangles are similar.

Janelle and Lamar are visiting their Aunt April and Uncle Mason. Aunt April has given each of them a section of the backyard in which to plant whatever they wish. Janelle wants to plant strawberries to sell at the local market. Lamar loves corn on the cob, and corn is what he wants to grow.

Janelle and Lamar can make their gardens any shape they wish. In preparation, they draw a sketch of their gardens including brick borders. They then purchase materials and discuss how to outline their gardens with bricks. However, Lamar is having trouble laying out his border; there aren't enough bricks. "Well, it should work. My design is the same as Janelle's but bigger. I took the measurements from her drawings and added 4 feet to each side. I even double-checked my measurements," he said.

Aunt April is trying to figure out what happened and looks at their gardens, "I think I know what went wrong. Here, let's look at some other garden shapes," Auntie says.

Help Janelle, Lamar, and Aunt April investigate different garden shapes to figure out why Lamar did not have enough bricks for his border.

How

- Make a copy of the garden shapes on page 106 and select one.

- Use a centimeter ruler to measure the length of each side. Write down the measurements.

- Now perform a ratio check. Remember that we are dividing the shortest leg by the longest leg to calculate the ratio. Record this ratio by the garden shape.

- Now let's make the garden bigger. Add 2.5 cm to the length of each side.

- Draw a new garden using these lengths.

- Describe to your partner how the new garden shape compares to the original.

- Now do a ratio check for the new garden and record it. Compare the two ratios to see if the shapes are similar.

- What would happen if you used multiplication instead of addition? Take your original garden and multiply the lengths by 2.5 cm.

- Create a third garden using the new lengths.

- Do your gardens look the same? How can you be sure? Do a ratio check and jot it down.

- Now you have three garden shapes. As you and your partner compare all three shapes, what have you learned? Can you determine if the gardens are similar just by looking at them? What is the most accurate way to compare the gardens? Discuss your findings with your partner.

- Did you and your partner discover why Lamar didn't have enough bricks to outline his garden? Talk together and make sure you agree.

Here's More. . .
- Try different shapes from page 106. Either add or multiply the lengths of each side by numbers of your choice. Keep a record of the ratios. Was what you learned previously still true for the new garden shapes? Discuss your thinking with your partner.

- Select a different shape from page 106. What happens if you shrink a garden? Try subtracting or dividing garden lengths by 2.5 cm.

- How do your gardens compare when you add, subtract, multiply, or divide the side lengths? When are the shapes similar, and when are they not?

Garden SHAPES

TABLETOP TESSELLATIONS

We suggest that you try Make Your Garden Bigger *on page 103 before beginning this activity.*

Why is this important?

Geometry is often difficult for children because they do not have experience visualizing the relationships of objects in space.

In the middle grades, children investigate transformations. A transformation moves a geometric shape by flipping, sliding, and rotating it—without changing its angle measurements and side lengths. The more experiences your child has with transformations, the easier it will be for her to understand these actions in formal geometry.

In this activity, you and your child will create tabletop designs using the shapes on page 127. Your child will flip, slide, and rotate geometric objects without changing their size and shape. This will help build a foundation for making transformations on a coordinate grid, found in the *How Did I Get There?* activity on page 109.

MATERIALS
Geometric Shapes,
   page 127
pencils

Miho and James are tiling a tabletop as a project for the Boys and Girls Club in their neighborhood. They decided to use triangles, trapezoids, and parallelograms in their patterns. Let's help Miho and James create three tabletop designs.

How

- Make a copy of the geometric shapes on page 127 and cut them out.

- Choose one of the shapes to tile your tabletop. Place the shape in the center and trace around it.

- Flip, slide, or rotate the shape so that at least one side completely matches your last piece.

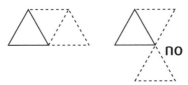

• Continue tracing your design as you cover the tabletop.

• You will use a combination of flips, slides, and rotations to create your design. Cover as much of your tabletop as possible. There may be some pieces that overlap the edge of the table. When this happens, trace as much of the shape as you can.

• When you are finished, record how many times the shape was flipped, slid, and rotated.

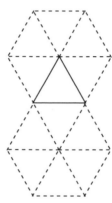

Your designs are called tessellations *because you cover a flat surface (the tabletop) with a repeated pattern that does not overlap or leave spaces uncovered.*

• Using the other shapes from page 127, create two other tabletop designs for Miho and James. Make sure you record the number of flips, slides, and rotations for each design.

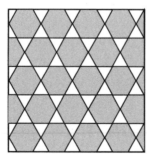 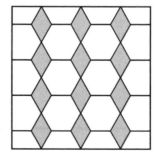 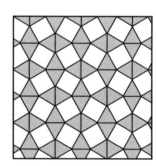

HOW DID I GET THERE?

We suggest that you and your child complete Tabletop Tessellations *on page 107 before beginning this activity.*

Why is this important?

Transformations are used in many careers such as computer graphics, architecture, and engineering. A transformation moves a geometric shape without changing its angle measurements or side lengths.

In *Tabletop Tessellations,* your child created designs using transformations (slides, flips, and rotations). In this activity, you and your child will determine how a figure is transformed to a new location on a coordinate grid.

MATERIALS

pencils

tracing paper or other
   transparent paper

Coordinate grids #2
   and #3, pages 111–112

Coordinate Grid Paper,
   page 124

How Did I Get There?
   Cards, pages 114–115

How

• Now let's take a closer look at what happens when we move a shape on a coordinate grid. Special Note: For your convenience, we included coordinate grid paper on page 124. You may copy and use it instead of writing in the book.

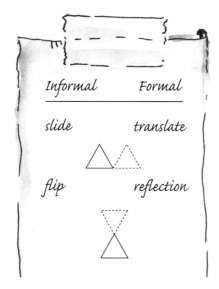

Translation (a slide)

- Coordinate Grid 1 shows what happens when we translate (slide) figure ABCD five (5) units to the right. The translated figure is read A prime, B prime, C prime, D prime or A' B' C' D'. Notice that point A prime is 5 units from point A, B prime is 5 units from B, C prime is 5 units from C, and D prime is 5 units from D.

GRID 1

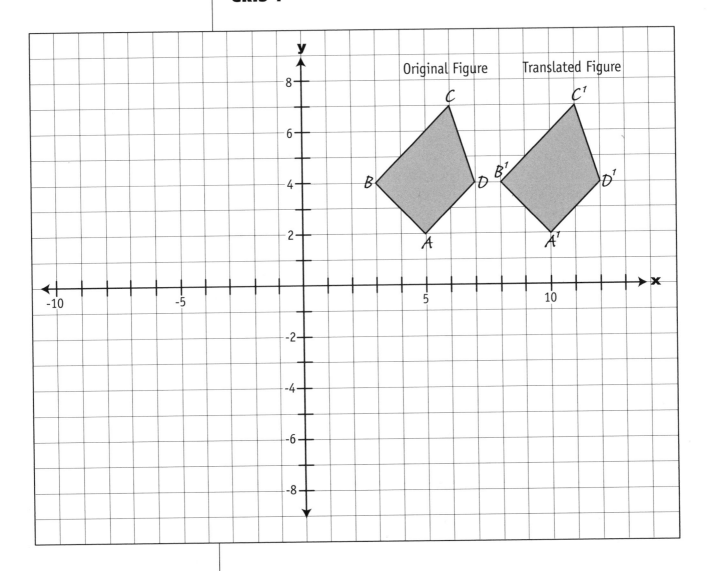

Now you and your child can practice translating (sliding) this shape. Using Grid 2, translate figure EFGH eight (8) units to the right. Label the new figure E' F' G' H'.

GRID 2

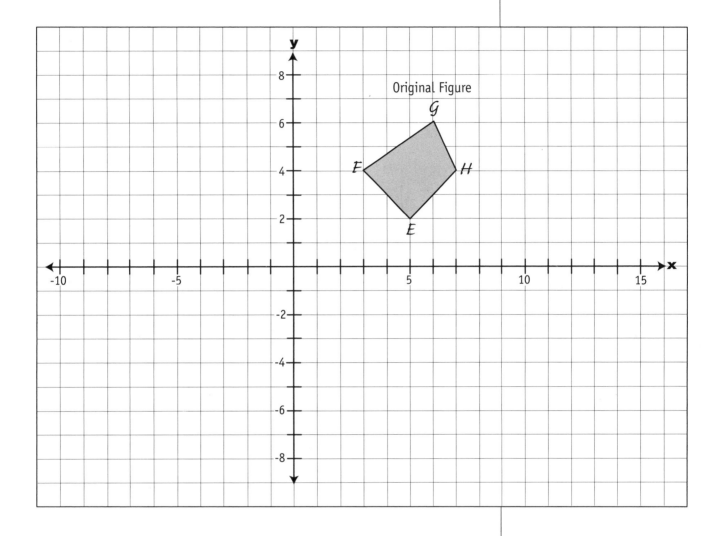

Reflection (a flip)

- Now try a reflection on Grid 3. Using a piece of tracing paper large enough to cover the entire grid, carefully trace figure IJKL. Be sure to also trace the horizontal and vertical axes.

- Fold the tracing paper along the vertical axis. Line up the vertical line on your tracing paper with that on the grid so that the figure on your paper lies to the left of figure IJKL.

- Go over your shape with a pencil so you can see the imprint on the co-ordinate grid. Remove the tracing paper and trace over the imprinted figure.

- Now you have a reflection. Label this figure I' J' K' L'.

GRID 3

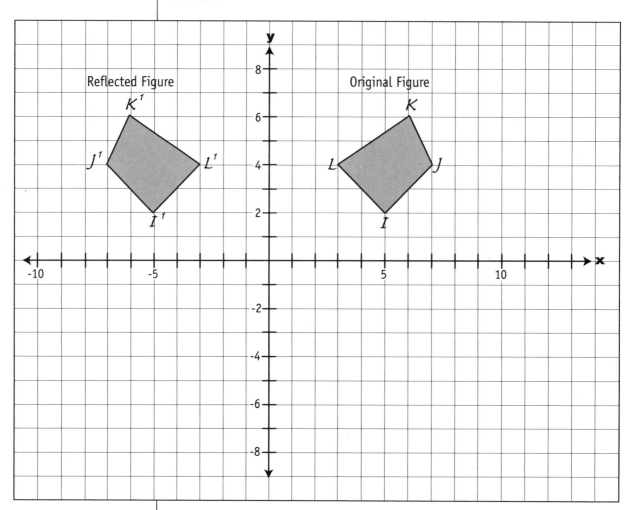

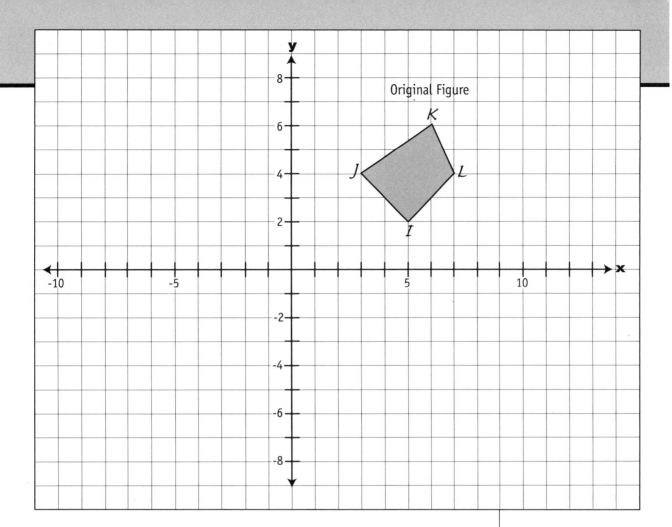

How Did I Get There?

- Each figure on the How Did I Get There cards has been translated and/or reflected from one location on the coordinate grid to another.

- Using the information you learned, determine how the original figure on each card was shifted to the new location. Figures were moved horizontally or vertically only. Record the type of movement on each card. See example Card 1 on page 114.

Suggestions

- What are the coordinate points of the original figure?

- Do the two figures lie on the same horizontal or vertical line?

- Are the letters on each figure in the same position?

- Is the figure orientated in the same direction as the original?

- It may be helpful to trace or cut out the original figure and physically move it along the coordinate lines to determine how the original figure was translated and/or reflected.

How Did I Get There CARDS

Card 1

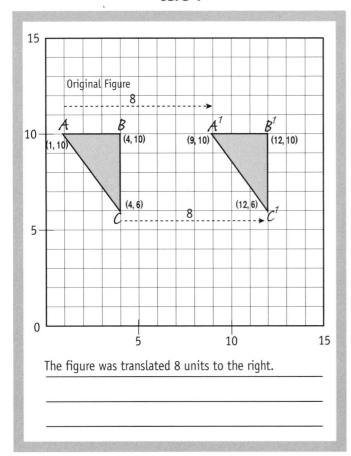

The figure was translated 8 units to the right.

Card 2

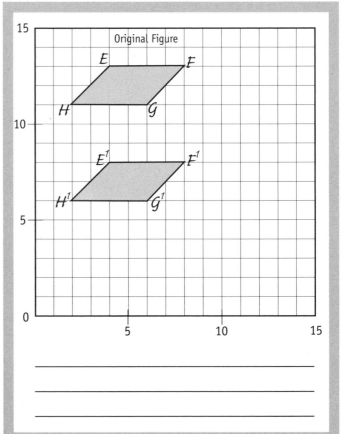

Card 3

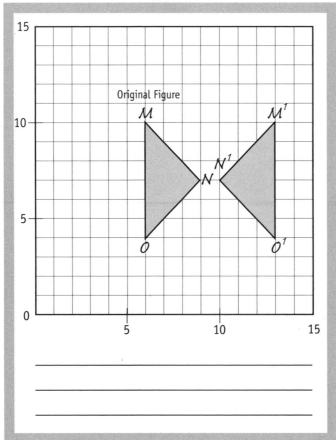

How Did I Get There CARDS

Card 4

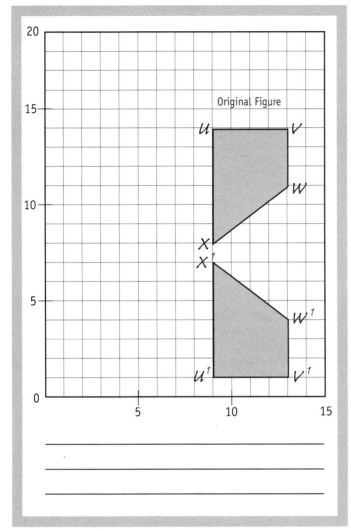

Card 5

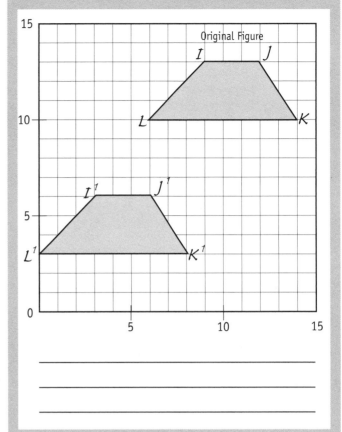

Card 6

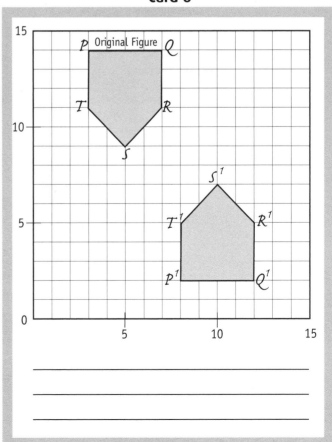

Note: Descriptions for all job titles are not included. Please consult EQUALS website **www.lawrencehallofscience/equals/edu** or the Bureau of Labor Statistics, under Occupational Outlook Handbook, **http://www.bls.gov/search/ooh.asp?ct=OOH** for more job descriptions or updated salary information.

Accountant I (Accounting)

Responsible for completion and maintenance of general ledgers and financial reports. May require a bachelor's degree in accounting and 0–2 years of experience in the field or in a related area. Has knowledge of commonly used concepts, practices, and procedures within a particular field. Relies on instructions and pre-established guidelines to perform the functions of the job. Works under immediate supervision. Primary job functions do not typically require exercising independent judgment. Typically reports to a supervisor or manager.

A typical Accountant I earns a median base salary of $35,722.

Accountant I

25th percentile	Median	75th percentile
$32,191	$35,722	$39,574

Animal Technician (Science and Research)

Responsible for the daily care of research animals. Requires a high school diploma with 0–2 years of experience in the field or in a related area. Has knowledge of commonly used concepts, practices, and procedures within a particular field. Relies on instructions and pre-established guidelines to perform the functions of the job. Works under immediate supervision. Primary job functions do not typically require exercising independent judgment. Typically reports to a supervisor or manager.

A typical Animal Technician earns a median base salary of $26,795.

Animal Technician

25th percentile	Median	75th percentile
$25,810	$26,795	$29,842

Appraiser—Commercial Real Estate (Insurance)

Examines and evaluates commercial property to establish a fair market value for loan collateral. Requires a high school diploma or its equivalent and 6–8 years of related experience. Familiar with standard concepts, practices, and procedures within a particular field. Relies on experience and judgment to plan and accomplish goals. Performs a variety of tasks. A certain degree of creativity and latitude is required. Typically reports to a manager or head of a unit/department.

A typical Appraiser (Commercial Real Estate) earns a median base salary of $68,919.

Appraiser

25th percentile	Median	75th percentile
$66,930	$68,919	$75,945

Architectural Drafter I (Graphic Arts)

Conceives, designs, plans, and constructs models for new or modified structures. May be responsible for coordinating and determining quantity and types of materials, while planning sequences for ordering materials. May require an associate's degree in related area and 0–2 years of experience in the field or in a related area. Has knowledge of commonly used concepts, practices, and procedures within a particular field. Relies on instructions and pre-established guidelines to perform the functions of the job. Works under immediate supervision. Primary job functions do not typically require exercising independent judgment. Typically reports to a supervisor or manager.

A typical Architectural Drafter I earns a median base salary of $27,217.

Architectural Drafter I

25th percentile	Median	75th percentile
$23,181	$27,217	$33,152

Astronomer (Science and Research)

Studies, researches, and analyzes celestial phenomena. Develops methodologies to solve problems in physics and mathematics. May require an advanced degree and at least 2–4 years of direct experience in the field. A Ph.D. is required for research and development positions. Familiar with a variety of the field's concepts, practices, and procedures. Relies on limited experiences and judgment to plan and accomplish goals. Performs a variety of tasks. A wide degree of creativity and latitude is expected.

A typical Astronomer earns a median base salary of $80,447.

Astronomer

25th percentile	Median	75th percentile
$79,168	$80,447	$92,826

Attorney I (Legal Services)

Prepares and examines contracts involving leases, licenses, purchases, sales, insurance, etc. Provides legal advice to an organization and participates in major legal actions. Must be a graduate of an accredited law school with 0–3 years of experience.

A typical Attorney I earns a median base salary of $72,175.

Attorney I

25th percentile	Median	75th percentile
$62,471	$72,175	$81,490

Biochemist I (Science and Research)

Evaluates the physical properties of various living organisms in order to investigate their applications to medicine and other industries. Requires a bachelor's degree and 0–2 years of experience in the field or in a related area. Has knowledge of commonly used concepts, practices, and procedures within a particular field. Relies on instructions and pre-established guidelines to perform the functions of the job. Works under immediate supervision. Primary job functions do not typically require exercising independent judgment. Typically reports to a supervisor or manager.

A typical Biochemist I earns a median base salary of $37,627.

Biochemist I

25th percentile	Median	75th percentile
$33,257	$37,627	$43,983

Biologist I (Science and Research)

Studies the basic principles of plant and animal life and the effects of varying environmental and physical conditions. Requires a bachelor's degree and 0–2 years of experience in the field or in a related area. Has knowledge of commonly used concepts, practices, and procedures within a particular field. Relies on instructions and pre-established guidelines to perform the functions of the job. Works under immediate supervision. Primary job functions do not typically require exercising independent judgment. Typically reports to a supervisor or manager.

A typical Biologist I earns a median base salary of $33,213.

Biologist I

25th percentile	Median	75th percentile
$29,880	$33,213	$37,262

Bookkeeper (Accounting)

Maintains and records business transactions. Balances ledgers and prepares reports. May require an associate's degree or its equivalent with 2–4 years of experience in the field or in a related area. Familiar with standard concepts, practices, and procedures within a particular field. Relies on limited experience and judgment to plan and accomplish goals. Performs a variety of tasks. Works under general supervision. A certain degree of creativity and latitude is required. Typically reports to a manager or head of a unit/department.

A typical Bookkeeper earns a median base salary of $31,621.

Bookkeeper

25th percentile	Median	75th percentile
$27,254	$31,621	$36,155

Captain/Pilot in Command—Large Jet (Aviation and Airlines)

Ensures that trip of assigned flight (aircraft larger than 12,500 pounds at takeoff) is conducted in the safest manner possible. Possesses current airline transport certificate with necessary type ratings. Requires a minimum of 5,000 hours of flight experience.

A typical Captain/Pilot in Command (Large Jet) earns a median base salary of $85,755.

Captain/Pilot in Command

25th percentile	Median	75th percentile
$75,531	$85,755	$98,830

Carpenter I (Construction and Installation)

Inspects, repairs, installs, modifies, rebuilds, constructs, and maintains woodwork and other related structures. Requires a high school diploma or its equivalent with 0–2 years of experience in the field or in a related area. May have to complete an apprenticeship and/or formal training in area of specialty. Has knowledge of commonly used concepts, practices, and procedures within a particular field. Relies on instructions and pre-established guidelines to perform the functions of the job. Works under immediate supervision. Primary job functions do not typically require exercising independent judgment. Typically reports to a supervisor/manager.

A typical Carpenter I earns a median base salary of $29,066.

Carpenter I

25th percentile	Median	75th percentile
$25,198	$29,066	$34,667

Cashier, General (Accounting)

Receives and disburses money in establishments other than financial institutions. May also be responsible for processing credit card transactions. Requires a high school diploma or its equivalent with 0–2 years of experience in the field or in a related area. Has knowledge of commonly used concepts, practices, and procedures within a particular field. Relies on instructions and pre-established guidelines to perform the functions of the job. Works under immediate supervision. Primary job functions do not typically require exercising independent judgment. Typically reports to a supervisor or manager.

A typical Cashier, General earns a median base salary of $16,599.

Cashier, General

25th percentile	Median	75th percentile
$14,096	$16,599	$20,433

Chemist I (Pharmaceuticals)

Evaluates the chemical and physical properties of various organic and inorganic substances in order to investigate their applications to medicine and other industries. Requires a bachelor's degree and 0–2 years of experience in the field or in a related area. Has knowledge of commonly used concepts, practices, and procedures within a particular field. Relies on instructions and pre-established guidelines to perform the functions of the job. Works under immediate supervision. Primary job functions do not typically require exercising independent judgment. Typically reports to a supervisor or manager.

A typical Chemist I earns a median base salary of $37,984.

Chemist I

25th percentile	Median	75th percentile
$34,659	$37,984	$42,701

Construction and Building Inspector (Skilled and Trades)

Inspects and conducts plan reviews of residential/commercial construction and ensures the enforcement of property maintenance. May be expected to prepare written zoning, building, and mechanical plan reviews. May require an associate's degree or its equivalent and 2–4 years of experience in the field or in a related area. Familiar with standard concepts, practices, and procedures within a particular field. Relies on limited experience and judgment to plan and accomplish goals. Performs a variety of tasks. Works under general supervision. A certain degree of creativity and latitude is required. Typically reports to a supervisor/manager.

A typical Construction and Building Inspector earns a median base salary of $43,463.

Construction and Building Inspector

25th percentile	Median	75th percentile
$36,147	$43,463	$53,160

Data Control Clerk I (Administrative, Support, and Clerical)

Collects, reviews, and inputs data into a computer processing system; audits output data. May be expected to code data and input data for computer processing. Identifies and resolves production-related errors. Maintains and revises procedural lists, control records, and coding schemes to process source data. Requires a high school diploma or its equivalent and 0–3 years of experience in the field or in a related area. Has knowledge of commonly used concepts, practices, and procedures within a particular field. Relies on instructions and pre-established guidelines to perform the functions of the job. Works under immediate supervision. Primary job functions do not typically require exercising independent judgment. Typically reports to a supervisor.

A typical Data Control Clerk I earns a median base salary of $27,944.

Data Control Clerk I

25th percentile	Median	75th percentile
$24,467	$27,944	$31,152

Dental Hygienist (Healthcare — Practitioners)

Under the direct supervision of a dentist, cleans calcareous deposits, accretions, and stains from teeth and beneath margins of gums, using dental instruments. Feels lymph nodes under patient's chin to detect swelling or tenderness that could indicate presence of oral cancer. Feels and visually examines gums for sores and signs of disease. May provide clinical services and health education to improve and maintain oral health of school children. May conduct dental health clinics for community groups to augment services of dentist. May require an associate's degree or its equivalent and 2–4 years of experience and is licensed as a dental hygienist. Familiar with standard concepts, practices, and procedures within a particular field. Relies on limited experience and judgment to plan and accomplish goals. Performs a variety of tasks. Works under general supervision; typically reports to a dentist. A certain degree of creativity and latitude is required.

A typical Dental Hygienist earns a median base salary of $45,745.

Dental Hygienist

25th percentile	Median	75th percentile
$39,200	$45,745	$52,775

Dentist (Healthcare—Practitioners)

Diagnoses and treats diseases, injuries, malformations of teeth and gums, and related oral structures. Requires a degree in dentistry from an accredited school of dentistry, and is licensed to practice dentistry. May require 2–4 years of experience. Familiar with standard concepts, practices, and procedures within a particular field. Relies on limited experience and judgment to plan and accomplish goals. Performs a variety of tasks. Works under general supervision. A wide degree of creativity and latitude is required.

A typical Dentist earns a median base salary of $102,968.

Dentist

25th percentile	Median	75th percentile
$82,624	$102,968	$123,990

Economist—Corporate (Financial Services)

Conducts research and analysis on economic data and trends and makes recommendations. Requires a bachelor's degree in a related field and at least 2–4 years of experience. Typically reports to a senior manager. A certain degree of creativity and latitude is required.

A typical Economist (Corporate) earns a median base salary of $79,159.

Economist

25th percentile	Median	75th percentile
$66,079	$79,159	$100,358

Electric/Electronics Technician I (Skilled and Trades)

Constructs, maintains, and tests electrical systems and components. Requires a high school diploma or its equivalent. May be required to complete an apprenticeship and/or formal training in area of specialty. May require 0–3 years of experience in the field or in a related area. Has knowledge of commonly used concepts, practices, and procedures within a particular field. Relies on instructions and pre-established guidelines to perform the functions of the job. Works under immediate supervision. Primary job functions do not typically require exercising independent judgment. Typically reports to a supervisor or manager.

A typical Electric/Electronics Technician I earns a median base salary of $33,450.

Electric/Electronics Technician I

25th percentile	Median	75th percentile
$29,901	$33,450	$37,063

Engineer I (Construction and Installation)

Responsible for design, development, implementation, and analysis of technical products and systems. Performs engineering design evaluations. May develop a range of products. Requires a bachelor's degree in engineering and 0–3 years of experience in the field or in a related area.

Has knowledge of commonly used concepts, practices, and procedures within a particular field. Relies on instructions and pre-established guidelines to perform the functions of the job. Works under immediate supervision. Typically reports to a supervisor or manager.

A typical Engineer I earns a median base salary of $50,839.

Engineer I

25th percentile	Median	75th percentile
$45,626	$50,839	$58,307

Estimator (Construction and Installation)

Forecasts project costs. Helps determine necessary resources for projects based on cost estimates. May require a bachelor's degree in a related field and 0–2 years of experience. Has knowledge of commonly used concepts, practices, and procedures within a particular field. Relies on instructions and pre-established guidelines to perform the functions of the job. Works under immediate supervision. Primary job functions do not typically require exercising independent judgment. Typically reports to a supervisor or manager.

A typical Estimator earns a median base salary of $34,474.

Estimator

25th percentile	Median	75th percentile
$30,026	$34,474	$43,371

Forester (Environment)

Manages and develops forest lands and resources for economic and recreational purposes. May require a bachelor's degree in a related area and at least 7 years of experience in the field or in a related area. Familiar with standard concepts, practices, and procedures within a particular field. Relies on experience and judgment to plan and accomplish goals. Performs a variety of complicated tasks. Generally manages exempt and nonexempt employees. Typically reports to the head of a unit/department. A wide degree of creativity and latitude is expected.

A typical Forester earns a median base salary of $51,026.

Forester

25th percentile	Median	75th percentile
$42,278	$51,026	$61,402

Geologist I (Energy and Utilities)

Researches the formation, dissolution, and content of rock layers. Researches the effects of internal pressures, heat, water, and erosion. Requires a bachelor's degree and 0–2 years of experience in the field or in a related area. Has knowledge of commonly used concepts, practices, and procedures within a particular field. Relies on instructions and pre-established guidelines to perform the functions of the job. Works under immediate supervision. Primary job functions do not typically require exercising independent judgment. Typically reports to a supervisor or manager.

A typical Geologist I earns a median base salary of $37,021.

Geologist I

25th percentile	Median	75th percentile
$34,579	$37,021	$39,890

High School Teacher (Education)

Prepares lesson plans and instructs adolescents. Evaluates and monitors student's performance. Requires a bachelor's degree and 2–4 years of experience in the field or in a related area. Some states require that teachers be certified. Familiar with standard concepts, practices, and procedures within a particular field. Relies on limited experience and judgment to plan and accomplish goals. Performs a variety of tasks. Works under general supervision; typically reports to the principal. A certain degree of creativity and latitude is required. Note: median base salary figures represent teachers with 15 years of experience.

A typical High School Teacher earns a median base salary of $44,709.

High School Teacher

25th percentile	Median	75th percentile
$35,425	$44,709	$52,516

Insurance Agent (Sales)

Sells insurance to new and current clients. May require an associate's degree with at least 2 years of experience in the field or in a related area. Familiar with standard concepts, practices, and procedures within a particular field. Relies on limited experience and judgment to plan and accomplish goals. Performs a variety of tasks. Works under general supervision; typically reports to a supervisor or manager. A degree of creativity and latitude is expected.

A typical Insurance Agent earns a median base salary of $36,214.

Insurance Agent

25th percentile	Median	75th percentile
$33,074	$36,214	$40,851

Interior Designer (Architecture)

Develops the interior design of various building types including private homes and public buildings. May require a bachelor's degree or its equivalent and 0–2 years of experience in the field or in a related area. Familiar with standard concepts, practices, and procedures within a particular field. Relies on experience and judgment to plan and accomplish goals. Performs a variety of complicated tasks. Typically reports to a supervisor/manager. A wide degree of creativity and latitude is expected.

A typical Interior Designer earns a median base salary of $30,132.

Interior Designer

25th percentile	Median	75th percentile
$28,593	$30,132	$35,779

Jeweler (Skilled and Trades)

Fabricates and repairs jewelry articles such as rings, brooches, pendants, bracelets, and lockets. Requires a high school diploma or its equivalent. May have to complete an apprenticeship and/or formal training in area of specialty with 0–2 years of experience in the field or in a related area. Familiar with standard concepts, practices, and procedures within a particular field. Relies on limited experience and judgment to plan and accomplish goals. Performs a variety of tasks. Works under general supervision; typically reports to a supervisor or manager. A certain degree of creativity and latitude is expected.

A typical Jeweler earns a median base salary of $29,897.

Jeweler

25th percentile	Median	75th percentile
$24,228	$29,897	$37,256

Land Surveyor I (Construction and Installation)

Surveys and investigates land surfaces to project precise measurement and location of lines, angles, points, areas, and elevations. Performs project research and boundary calculations; and records accuracy of survey data, notes, and sketches. May require a high school diploma or its equivalent with 0–2 years experience in the field. May have to complete an apprenticeship, and/or formal training in area of specialty. Has knowledge of commonly used concepts, practices, and procedures within a particular field. Relies on instructions and pre-established guidelines to perform the functions of the job. Works under immediate supervision. Typically reports to a supervisor/manager.

A typical Land Surveyor I earns a median base salary of $28,461.

Land Surveyor I

25th percentile	Median	75th percentile
$23,849	$28,461	$33,380

Loan Review Officer I (Financial Services)

Performs reviews of bank's loans to ensure compliance with established policies and standards. May require a bachelor's degree in area of specialty and 3–5 years of experience in the field or in a related area. Familiar with a variety of the field's concepts, practices, and procedures. Relies on extensive experience and judgment to plan and accomplish goals. Performs a variety of tasks. May lead and direct the work of others. A wide degree of creativity and latitude is expected. Typically reports to a manager or head of a unit/department.

A typical Loan Review Officer I earns a median base salary of $38,010.

Loan Review Officer I

25th percentile	Median	75th percentile
$32,550	$38,010	$42,870

Machinist I (Skilled and Trades)

Assembles, repairs, and fabricates metal parts by operating mechanical equipment. Requires a high school diploma or its equivalent. May be required to meet certain certifications in field and to have at least 0–2 years of experience. Has knowledge of commonly used concepts, practices, and procedures within a particular field. Relies on instructions and pre-established guidelines to perform the functions of the job. Works under immediate supervision. Primary job functions do not typically require exercising independent judgment. Typically reports to a supervisor/manager.

A typical Machinist I earns a median base salary of $28,827.

Machinist I

25th percentile	Median	75th percentile
$25,737	$28,827	$32,663

Mathematician (Science and Research)

Solves scientific and engineering problems. Applies mathematical theories to new areas of scientific investigation. Requires a bachelor's degree in a related area and 3–5 years of experience in the field or in a related area. Familiar with standard concepts, practices, and procedures within a particular field. Relies on limited experience and judgment to plan and accomplish goals to perform a variety of tasks. Works under general supervision; typically reports to a supervisor or manager. A certain degree of creativity and latitude is required.

A typical Mathematician earns a median base salary of $69,010.

Mathematician

25th percentile	Median	75th percentile
$54,430	$69,010	$82,212

Mechanic Technician I (Skilled and Trades)

Constructs, maintains, and tests mechanical equipment, machinery, and components. Requires a high school diploma or its equivalent. May be required to complete an apprenticeship and/or formal training in area of specialty. May require 0–2 years of experience in the field or in a related area. Has knowledge of commonly used concepts, practices, and procedures within a particular field. Relies on instructions and pre-established guidelines to perform the functions of the job. Works under immediate supervision. Primary job functions do not typically require exercising independent judgment. Typically reports to a supervisor or manager.

A typical Mechanic Technician I earns a median base salary of $29,859.

Mechanic Technician I

25th percentile	Median	75th percentile
$26,115	$29,859	$34,405

Medical Records Administrator

Coordinates personnel that handle permanent medical records of patients by analyzing, coding, indexing, and storing the records. Ensures that records are complete, accurate, and adhere to standards. May require an associate's degree or its equivalent with 2–4 years of experience in the field or in a related area. Must also be a registered records administrator (RRA). Familiar with standard concepts, practices, and procedures within a particular field. Relies on experience and judgment to plan and accomplish goals. Performs a variety of tasks. Works under general supervision. A certain degree of creativity and latitude is required. Typically reports to a manager or head of a unit/department.

A typical Medical Records Administrator earns a median base salary of $50,254.

Medical Records Administrator

25th percentile	Median	75th percentile
$39,571	$50,254	$63,381

Operating Systems Programmer I (IT — Computers, Software)

Reviews, analyzes, develops, installs, and modifies computer operating systems. Analyzes and resolves problems associated with operating systems. Detects, diagnoses, and reports related problems. May require an associate's degree or its equivalent and 0–2 years of experience in the field or in a related area. Has knowledge of commonly used concepts, practices, and procedures within a particular field. Relies on instructions and pre-established guidelines to perform the functions of the job. Works under immediate supervision. Primary job functions do not typically require exercising independent judgment. Typically reports to a project leader or manager.

A typical Operating Systems Programmer I earns a median base salary of $43,995.

Operating Systems Programmer I

25th percentile	Median	75th percentile
$39,119	$43,995	$48,987

Optometrist (Healthcare — Practitioners)

Oversees the patient's diagnosis, treatment, and prevention of vision problems and diseases. Requires a degree in medicine from an accredited school of optometry, and is licensed to practice optometry. May require at least 2–4 years of clinical experience in optometry. Familiar with standard concepts, practices, and procedures within a particular field. Relies on experience and judgment to plan and accomplish goals. Performs a variety of tasks. May report to a medical director. A wide degree of creativity and latitude is expected.

A typical Optometrist earns a median base salary of $74,028.

Optometrist

25th percentile	Median	75th percentile
$68,822	$74,028	$88,980

Order Clerk (Administrative, Support, and Clerical)

Receives and processes orders for materials and merchandise. Requires a high school diploma or its equivalent with 0–2 years of experience in the field or in a related area. Has knowledge of commonly used concepts, practices, and procedures within a particular field. Relies on instructions and pre-established guidelines to perform the functions of the job. Works under immediate supervision. Primary job functions do not typically require exercising independent judgment. Typically reports to a supervisor or manager.

A typical Order Clerk earns a median base salary of $26,382.

Order Clerk

25th percentile	Median	75th percentile
$22,401	$26,382	$29,042

Physical Therapist (Healthcare – Practitioners)

Plans and directs a course of physical therapy to restore motor control. Requires a master's degree and is certified as a physical therapist with 2–4 years of clinical experience. Familiar with standard concepts, practices, and procedures within a particular field. Relies on limited experience and judgment to plan and accomplish goals. Performs a variety of tasks. Typically reports to a manager or supervisor. A certain degree of creativity and latitude is required.

A typical Physical Therapist earns a median base salary of $57,602.

Physical Therapist

25th percentile	Median	75th percentile
$50,434	$57,602	$61,927

Physician (Healthcare — Practitioners)

Oversees the patient's diagnosis, treatment, and prevention of illnesses and/or injury. Requires a degree in medicine from an accredited school of medicine, and is licensed to practice medicine. May require 2–4 years of clinical experience. Familiar with standard concepts, practices, and procedures within a particular field. Relies on experience and judgment to plan and accomplish goals. Performs a variety of tasks. May report to a medical director. A wide degree of creativity and latitude is expected.

A typical Physician earns a median base salary of $125,036.

Physician

25th percentile	Median	75th percentile
$86,609	$125,036	$154,914

Physicist I (Science and Research)

Researches subjects such as mechanics, heat, light, sound, electricity, pneumatics, magnetism, and radiation. Develops laws and theories of physics for their application to industry. Requires a bachelor's degree and 0–2 years of experience in the field or in a related area. Has knowledge of commonly used concepts, practices, and procedures within a particular field. Relies on instructions and pre-established guidelines to perform the functions of the job. Works under immediate supervision. Primary job functions do not typically require exercising independent judgment. Typically reports to a supervisor or manager.

A typical Physicist I earns a median base salary of $42,978.

Physicist I

25th percentile	Median	75th percentile
$40,593	$42,978	$46,913

Professor (Education)

Teaches core courses in a specialized discipline and conducts original empirical research. Provides mentorship to doctoral students and junior professors in their specialized discipline. Requires a Ph.D. in the field of specialty and at least ten years of experience teaching and conducting scholarly research.

A typical Professor earns a median base salary of $95,146.

Professor

25th percentile	Median	75th percentile
$77,579	$95,146	$116,876

Psychologist (Healthcare — Practitioners)

Provides individual and group counseling services to assist individuals in their personal, social, educational, and vocational development and adjustment. May require a Ph.D. in psychology with at least 2–4 years of clinical experience in psychology. Familiar with standard concepts, practices, and procedures within a particular field. Relies on experience and judgment to plan and accomplish goals. Performs a variety of tasks. May report to a medical director. A wide degree of creativity and latitude is expected.

A typical Psychologist earns a median base salary of $48,898.

Psychologist

25th percentile	Median	75th percentile
$43,489	$48,898	$58,484

Respiratory Therapist (Healthcare —Technicians)

Assists in the diagnosis, treatment, and management of patients with pulmonary disorders. May require an associate's degree or its equivalent and 2–4 years of experience in the field or in a related area. May be expected to meet certain state certifications, and may be CPR certified. Familiar with standard concepts, practices, and procedures within a particular field. Relies on limited experience and judgment to plan and accomplish goals. Performs a variety of tasks. Works under general supervision; typically reports to a supervisor or manager. A certain degree of creativity and latitude is required.

A typical Respiratory Therapist earns a median base salary of $42,420.

Respiratory Therapist

25th percentile	Median	75th percentile
$38,784	$42,420	$46,290

Speech and Language Pathologist (Healthcare — Practitioners)

Diagnoses and treats speech and language problems, and engages in scientific study of human communication. Diagnoses and evaluates speech and language skills as related to educational, medical, social, and psychological factors. Plans, directs, or conducts rehabilitative treatment programs to restore communicative efficiency of individuals with communication problems. May require a master's degree in speech/language pathology and 0–2 years of experience in the field. Expected to meet certain state licensing requirements. Familiar with standard concepts, practices, and procedures within a particular field. Typically works under indirect supervision.

A typical Speech and Language Pathologist earns a median base salary of $51,371.

Speech and Language Pathologist

25th percentile	Median	75th percentile
$47,182	$51,371	$55,412

Statistician (Science and Research)

Analyzes and interprets data from various sources. Compiles reports, charts, and tables based on established statistical methods. Requires a bachelor's degree in a related area and 2–4 years of experience in the field or in a related area. Familiar with standard concepts, practices, and procedures within a particular field. Relies on limited experience and judgment to plan and accomplish goals. Performs a variety of tasks. Works under general supervision; typically reports to a supervisor or manager. A certain degree of creativity and latitude is required.

A typical Statistician earns a median base salary of $46,327.

Statistician

25th percentile	Median	75th percentile
$40,339	$46,327	$51,785

Stockbroker (Financial Services)

Markets company's products and/or services to prospects and clients. Assists clients in developing plans to achieve financial goals. Requires a bachelor's degree and experience in the field or in a related area. Must meet state licensing requirements and become a registered representative with the National Association of Securities Dealers, Inc. (NASD). Must also pass the Series 7 exam (General Securities Registered Representative Examination).

A typical Stockbroker earns a median base salary of $45,673.

Stockbroker

25th percentile	Median	75th percentile
$39,708	$45,673	$49,443

Stock Clerk (Administrative, Support, and Clerical)

Locates stock and delivers items to their destination upon request. Requires a high school diploma with 0–2 years experience. Typically reports to a supervisor or manager.

A typical Stock Clerk earns a median base salary of $23,447.

Stock Clerk

25th percentile	Median	75th percentile
$21,153	$23,447	$27,297

Teller I (Banking)

Processes a variety of routine financial transactions including check cashing, withdrawals, deposits, and loan payments. Responsible for managing and balancing cash drawer. Requires a high school diploma or equivalent and 0–1 years of experience.

A typical Teller I earns a median base salary of $20,009.

Teller I

25th percentile	Median	75th percentile
$18,450	$20,009	$21,688

Tool and Die Maker I (Skilled and Trades)

Builds and repairs machine shop tools. Requires a high school diploma or its equivalent. May be required to complete an apprenticeship and/or formal training in area of specialty with 0–2 years of experience in the field or in a related area. Has knowledge of commonly used concepts, practices, and procedures within a particular field. Relies on instructions and pre-established guidelines to perform the functions of the job. Works under immediate supervision. Primary job functions do not typically require exercising independent judgment. Typically reports to a supervisor or manager.

A typical Tool and Die Maker I earns a median base salary of $34,340.

Tool and Die Maker I

25th percentile	Median	75th percentile
$29,830	$34,340	$39,226

Travel Clerk
(Administrative, Support, and Clerical)

Provides basic travel information to customers inquiring about fares, routes, and accommodations. May require a high school diploma or its equivalent with 0–2 years of experience in the field or in a related area. Has knowledge of commonly used concepts, practices, and procedures within a particular field. Relies on instructions and pre-established guidelines to perform the functions of the job. Works under immediate supervision. Primary job functions do not typically require exercising independent judgment. Typically reports to a supervisor or manager.

A typical Travel Clerk earns a median base salary of $25,342.

Travel Clerk

25th percentile	Median	75th percentile
$23,700	$25,342	$28,735

Underwriter I — Property/Casualty (Insurance)

Analyzes inspection reports, location, risk, credit reports, etc., to accept or reject renewal/new property and casualty business. May require a bachelor's degree and 0–3 years of experience in the field or in a related area. Has knowledge of commonly used concepts, practices, and procedures within a particular field. Relies on instructions and pre-established guidelines to perform the functions of the job. Works under immediate supervision. Primary job functions do not typically require exercising independent judgment. Typically reports to a supervisor or manager.

A typical Underwriter I earns a median base salary of $40,654.

Underwriter I

25th percentile	Median	75th percentile
$37,910	$40,654	$43,622

Urban Planner

Develops land-use plans for the beneficial development of urban areas. Requires a bachelor's degree in a related field and 2–4 years of experience in the field or in a related area. Familiar with standard concepts, practices, and procedures within a particular field. Relies on judgment and limited experience to plan and accomplish goals. Performs a variety of tasks. Works under general supervision; typically reports to a supervisor or manager. A certain degree of creativity and latitude is required.

A typical Urban Planner earns a median base salary of $34,438.

Urban Planner

25th percentile	Median	75th percentile
$32,505	$34,438	$39,258

Veterinarian (Agriculture, Forestry, and Fishing)

Diagnoses and treats diseases and injuries of pets and farm animals. Requires a degree in veterinary medicine. Familiar with standard concepts, practices, and procedures within a particular field. Relies on limited experience and judgment to plan and accomplish goals. Performs a variety of tasks. A certain degree of creativity and latitude is required.

A typical Veterinarian earns a median base salary of $63,313.

Veterinarian

25th percentile	Median	75th percentile
$51,048	$63,313	$77,675

Weigher (Administrative, Support, and Clerical)

Measures and weighs materials to tally products. Requires a high school diploma or equivalent with 0–2 years experience. Typically reports to a supervisor or manager.

A typical Weigher earns a median base salary of $21,142.

Weigher

25th percentile	Median	75th percentile
$19,458	$21,142	$23,532

Welder I (Skilled and Trades)

Joins, fabricates, and repairs metal and other weldable material by applying appropriate welding techniques. Requires a high school diploma or its equivalent. May be required to complete an apprenticeship and/or formal training in area of specialty. May require 0–2 years of experience in the field or in a related area. Has knowledge of commonly used concepts, practices, and procedures within a particular field. Relies on instructions and pre-established guidelines to perform the functions of the job. Works under immediate supervision. Primary job functions do not typically require exercising independent judgment. Typically reports to a supervisor or manager.

A typical Welder I earns a median base salary of $27,626.

Welder I

25th percentile	Median	75th percentile
$22,994	$27,626	$33,704

Coordinate Grid PAPER

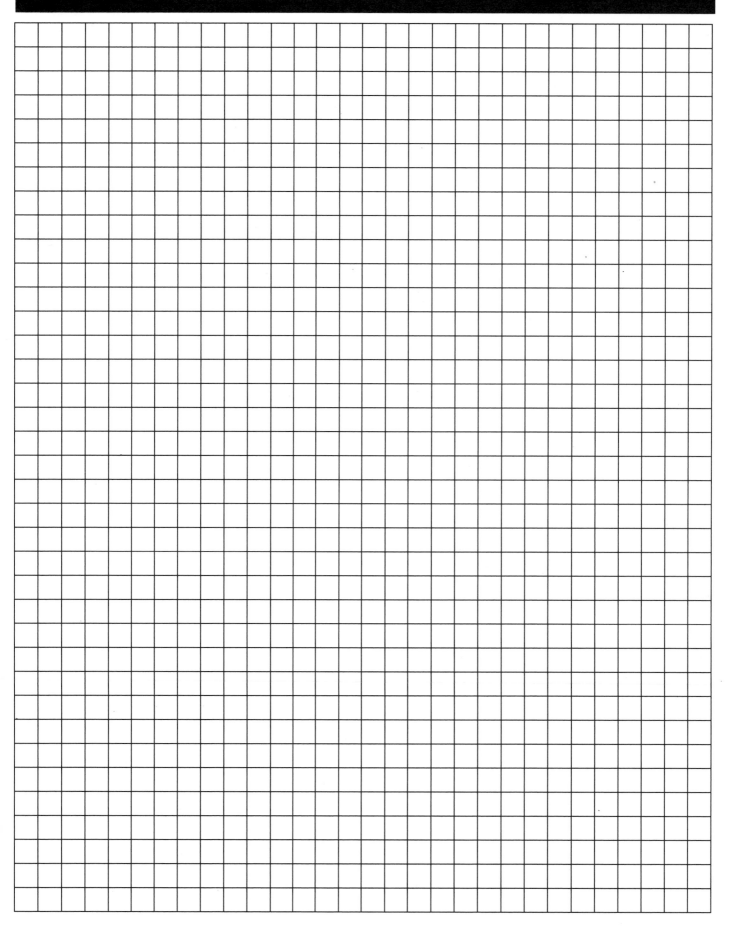

Square Grid PAPER

Triangle Grid PAPER

Geometric **SHAPES**

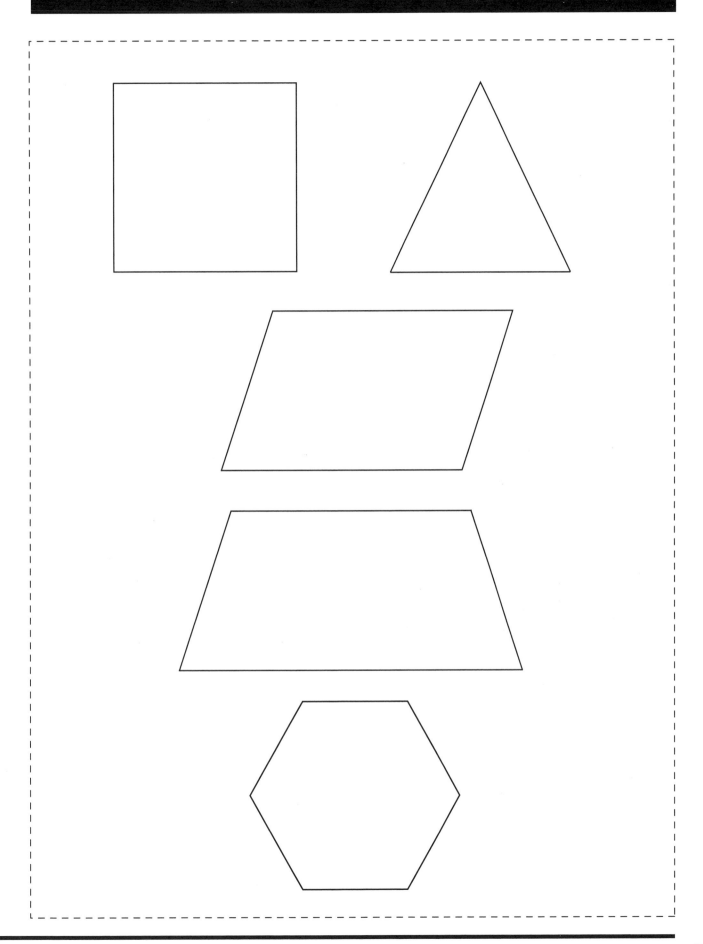

Index

U

V

W, X, Y, Z